AMAZON

How Amazon can m... y...

Esther Odejimi

To my beautiful family

Kenny, Enny

Thank you for your love, support, and encouragement
through the book writing process.

Table of Contents

Acknowledgments

My special gratitude goes to my creator and maker, God Almighty for sparing my life to complete this book. I'm also grateful to my Pastor (Mrs.) Harriet Giwa who encouraged me to complete this book and was always asking about the progress I was making. I will also like to appreciate my husband, Kenny for his moral support and encouragement during the writing of this book and making it a reality. My appreciation goes to other friends whose time will not permit me to mention their names here but have been wonderful contributor to the writing of this book, I'm grateful to you lots.

Disclaimer

The author has strived to be as accurate and complete as possible in the creation of this report, notwithstanding the fact that he does not warrant or represent at any time that the contents within are accurate due to the rapidly changing nature of the Internet.

While all attempts have been made to verify information provided in this publication, the Publisher assumes no responsibility for errors, omissions, or contrary interpretation of the subject matter herein. Any perceived slights of specific persons, peoples, or organizations are unintentional.

This book is a common sense guide to making money online using Amazon. In practical advice books, like anything else in life, there are no guarantees of income made. Readers are cautioned to rely on their own judgment about their individual circumstances to act accordingly. This book is not intended for use as a source of legal, business, accounting or financial advice. All readers are advised to seek services of competent professionals in legal, business, accounting, and finance field.

INTRODUCTION

This short book will be sharing the many ways anyone can make money from Amazon. There are three major areas that are sure ways to make money. There are others that you may investigate on the Amazon website.

The three main focus areas of this book are:

- Sell on Amazon
- Become an Affiliate
- Self-Publish with us (Kindle)

As of today, Amazon has become a household name when it comes to buying and selling. If you look at Amazon, you will see it has the following services where you can pick your interest areas in which to make money via amazon:

- Sell on Amazon
- Sell your services
- Sell your apps
- Become an affiliate
- Advertise your products
- Self-Publish with us
- Become an Amazon vendor

From the above options, individuals can choose which ones match natural skills to make you money. The age of internet has made it possible to connect the world as a global village and thus has made the idea of working from home more viable than it has ever been. You don't have to be in the United States or travel there before you do business with Americans nowadays; all that you need is connection to the internet.

Considering the many options for business, you might be wondering why you should choose Amazon out of all the other online marketplaces; this will become clearer as you read through this book. As of today, you can sell in any of the under listed Amazon markets, provided you reside in one of the countries where they allow third party sellers to sell on their platform. The main platform is in the United States, where they are headquartered. The other online selling platforms are:

- United Kingdom
- Australia
- Brazil
- Germany
- Spain
- Italy
- France
- Netherlands
- China
- India
- Japan
- Mexico
- Canada

To know more about countries that are allowed to register for selling on Amazon, check on the link below by copying and pasting into your web browser:

http://www.Amazon/gp/help/customer/display.html/ref=hp_rel_topic?ie=UTF8&nodeId=200417280

Have a look at the following scanned images as it relates to doing business with the online giants. However, please note that some of the services listed on the Amazon US portal are not available in other countries. You will have to review what is available where you live - but you may still be able to sell in other outlets that are only available in the US since Amazon allows this. (Also be aware that some of the countries are only into "self-publishing" as at the time of writing.)

Make Money with **amazon**.com

I'm interested in
SELLING ONLINE

Sell on Amazon
Sell your products to hundreds of millions of Amazon customers. No per-item listing fees.

+ Learn More

Amazon Payments
Bring the trusted Amazon payment experience to your website and make it easy for customers to pay.

+ Learn More

Amazon Advantage
Self-service consignment program to sell media products directly on Amazon.com.

+ Learn More

Fulfillment by Amazon
Leverage Amazon's fulfillment network, and we'll ship your orders for you.

+ Learn More

Amazon Vendor Express
Sell us your products and we take care of the rest—from promoting and shipping to customer service and returns.

+ Learn More

Amazon Local Register
Accept payments in person with a mobile phone or tablet. Low, flat rate. No hidden fees.

+ Learn More

I'm interested in
ADVERTISING ONLINE

Amazon Product Ads
Drive traffic from Amazon.com to products on your eCommerce website. Try it for free! Sign up and get $75 in free clicks[1].

+ Learn More

Amazon Display Ads
Reach your customers with display advertising on Amazon.com, mobile, and Kindle.

+ Learn More

I'm interested in
SELLING APPS

Amazon Appstore

Sell your Android apps on the Amazon Appstore and reach millions on Kindle Fire, Amazon Fire TV and select Android devices. It's easy to get started, over 75% of Android apps we tested work with no additional development necessary.

Amazon Monetization APIs

Monetize your apps and games by integrating the Amazon Mobile Ads API, In-App Purchasing API or the Mobile Associates API, which lets you sell physical products in your app and earn up to a 6% transaction fee.

Amazon HTML5 Web Apps

Sell your HTML5 apps and mobile optimized websites on the Amazon Web Appstore available in nearly 200 countries worldwide.

+ Learn More

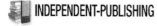
INDEPENDENT-PUBLISHING

Kindle Direct Publishing
Kindle Direct Publishing makes it fast and easy for you to independently publish your book for free and reach millions of Kindle and Kindle app reading customers worldwide.

+ Learn More

CreateSpace
CreateSpace helps you easily create, publish, and distribute your printed book to Amazon.com and Amazon's European websites for free.

+ Learn More

ACX
The Audiobook Creation Exchange (ACX) gives you control over audiobook production. Connect with a network of leading audiobook producers, or learn what you need to know to produce it yourself.

+ Learn More

AFFILIATE PROGRAM

Amazon Associates
Advertise Amazon products on your website and earn up to 15% in referral fees on the sale of books, music, DVDs, toys, electronics, kitchen, apparel, jewelry and more.

+ Learn More

What is buying and selling online?

This section will start explaining how to become registered as a seller on Amazon, explain what is meant by buying and selling on the internet. Simply put, it is an online e-commerce location where you buy products to sell on the internet. E-commerce is any trading in products or services using computer networks (such as the internet or commercial transactions conducted electronically on the internet).

There are so many ways you can participate in e-commerce. You can list the items you want to sell via online selling platforms like Amazon, eBay, Gumtree and more. This process requires you to be registered with any of the platforms so you can list your items for sale. Starting an online business can be exciting as you are opening yourself to a worldwide audience as alternative to opening a store within your area (which is only accessible to few people).

Selling online is much better than selling in a shop, restricted to passersby and people that live within your community. Selling online has a low set-up cost and you do not need much equipment or inventory to get started within a short period of time. The only major equipment that you need is:

- A PC
- A Broadband internet provider
- Google (search engine that is your friend at researching)

E-commerce business is simply what you can run from the comfort of your own home once you master the art. However, for you to really enjoy this market, you must research and identify the niche where you want to do business; otherwise, it can be challenging. This small book is thus written to guide you on how to start within a short period of time and to start well, too, reducing uncertainty and risk for your new business.

On the internet, there are thousands products that are being bought and sold in various categories, so you need to grab this chance, join the trend and start earning money. You have to learn a market, get to know it (preferably something you like or already know) and use your skills to dominate that category and beat your competitors. You will also need to learn the tools for selling, such as computer equipment. You can make huge profits by capitalizing on these differences if it is a niche that you know very well and like.

If you know details about computer equipment (like model, make, memory, go on the internet, do further research), then you can sell them and make a good profit. This is not only for computers, but for any product that you consider: baby products, beauty, health, appliances, clothing, video games, jewelry and much more. If you are a beginner, you will need to stick to just one niche - one step at a time, become a master, make money and then you can begin to add other niches.

Always stay on top of your market by doing frequent research on market prices change or the product itself. You can only make a profit if you stay on top of the trends.

Why sell on Amazon?

Unquestionably, the biggest e-commerce platform in the world is Amazon, which is an internet giant with global presence and reach. The company began as an online seller of books, but quickly adopted emerging trends and branched out into other areas such as sales of entertainment media (like DVDs, VHSs, CDs, online video and mp3 streaming and downloads, software and video games).

Amazon also expanded to other categories (electronics, clothing items, food, toys, children's items, jewelry, household items and more). Some years ago, Amazon diversified into the production of consumer electronics including the Kindle E-book reader, Kindle Fire Tablets, Fire TV and the Fire Phone.

The Business Model

Amazon allows both individuals and businesses to sell products through its many websites in different countries. Both individual and professional sellers manage all aspects of their selling via its Seller Central websites. From seller central, you can add products, inventory, manage orders and payments.

The Benefits

Higher Sales: Given the incredible scale, success and excellent customer service of Amazon as a marketplace, there are more chances of selling more products at better prices than most other online marketplaces. In addition, there are no listing fees compared to other marketplaces - you also may not need to take photos of your items if the same or similar ones are already selling on Amazon.

Access to Customers: More than 10 million customers visit Amazon sites on a daily basis to look for items to buy. While it is true that visitors will not be looking for your store in particular, they might actually search for the item you are selling. The customer could simply add it as one of their purchases. Your item would not be noticed if not for Amazon. Once you are able to get a customer, you convert the buyer into a repeat customer by offering a great product and quality customer service.

Infrastructure: In the Amazon marketplace, buyers get a variety of options and a better shopping experience. In addition, a single stream checkout and support helps create a smooth shopping experience.

Selling in Multiple Platforms: As a seller on Amazon, you can sell in multiple marketplaces and this will ensure you make money on different country platforms. Listing of your items is basically the same in one platform as in another.

Access a new sales channel: Selling your products via your own e-commerce site likely doesn't reach as many customers as an international selling location. In the United States alone, Amazon has over 95 million monthly unique visitors and by signing up in the US, it will enable you to sell on both U.S. and Canadian marketplaces. My advice to you, however, is if you are just starting, concentrate your selling efforts in the country where you live. You can expand to the other marketplaces once you learn the process very well.

Revolutionize your business: When you sell on Amazon with "Fulfillment by Amazon" (FBA), they will handle the heavy lifting for you. FBA is an optional service where you ship all your items to its warehouse, they will store your products, ship your orders when a buyer makes a purchase, manage customer service, returns and this will give you time to focus on growing your business. FBA will be a chapter on its own in this book.

In a nutshell, the major benefits of selling on Amazon are:

- Your products are easier to find and buy
- Convenient, trusted shopping experience for customers
- Security and fraud protection for you and your customers
- Sell your products in most of Amazon marketplaces
- Expose your products to millions of Amazon shoppers
- Access to Fulfillment by Amazon
- No product listing fees as in eBay
- Promote the products you sell on Amazon through keyword targeted ads with Amazon Sponsored Products Ads.

SELLING ON AMAZON - YOUR NEW BUSINESS

Decide what you want to sell

As a new seller, you can sell in at least 20 different categories. The number of items you are allowed to sell will depend on whether you sign up as an "individual" or "professional". Please read more about these on Amazon's website where you hope to sign up.

Sell what is already selling

Don't try to reinvent the wheel as it will amount to a wasted effort. Just go straight to the source, Amazon and check how well an item is selling. For instance, if you are thinking of selling a yoga mat, simply type the word into the search bar and see which results are available. You will like to see the top result with a "Best Sellers Rank" (BSR) of 2,000 or less. It is also good if the top three results are under 5,000. To find the BSR, click on the product page and scroll down to the area "Product Details." There, details will be listed related to shipping weight, average customer reviews, best sellers rank and more. To make an informed decision, open an excel worksheet where you can input the items as you research items to sell. If the item does not pass your test, delete it from your spreadsheet as an option to sell and move on to something else.

Your steps to finding the perfect product

Choose the right category

You will do yourself a favour when choosing your first product by choosing the right category - especially by choosing a product with which you are familiar. Make sure you choose one of the beginner-friendly categories as listed below as they do not require approval from Amazon:

- Sports and Outdoors
- Home & Kitchen
- Patio, Lawn and Garden
- Pet Supplies
- Baby

- Electronics
- Musical Instruments

Small, lightweight

For your first product, you do not want to mess with anything classified by Amazon as oversized, which means items that you sell must not be more than 20lbs (ideally less than 5lbs). It will be costly to store and ship, even if you use FBA. Another reason for this is that Amazon charges higher fees for oversized items with regard to picking, packing and handling.

Simple, not easily breakable

Choose an item that is simple and not easily breakable (like a yoga mat). Things that break easily (like glasses) can easily break, thus leading to losses. I am talking from experience because I have been there, which is why taking this advice will save you a lot of hassles.

Moderate price range

If you want to be able to sell your product easily and quickly, then your item should be priced between £10 - £40. If you sell at price below £10, you will not be left with enough profit after Amazon takes their portion. An item greater than £40 poses a few different inconveniences: sales are often lower because there is less impulse purchases; people want to know more about brands that cost more money, and; higher priced items tend to be recognized household brands).

Avoid patented products

If you want a long term business, do not go after patented products to avoid you getting your fingers burnt. You need to do things by the book. But how do you know? Amazon lists it in the product description on the website. You can also do google search for the product name including the word "patent" at the end of the word just to be sure.

Create a list of ideas

Once you have decided on the item you will be selling, you need to start brainstorming. Try to create a list of between 30 - 50 products, and you can make it juicy by using two spots to create your list. With Amazon, use the bestsellers and drill down into the categories by clicking the sub-categories, drill deeper and deeper. You can also watch other Amazon sellers by finding a seller you think is selling a private label product. Go to the seller's storefront by clicking on the seller's name and this will take you to all the items that this particular seller is selling on Amazon. Other sites that you can get ideas from is eBay, Pinterest and this site also http://www.trendhunter.com.

Assess the Competition

You must assess the market category in which you want to be selling. Look at overall number of sellers, the number of reviews and the quality of their listings. Most often than not, you can still sell in a category that has a vast number of sellers if you can do due diligence by looking at the quality of their listings. Use two-star reviews to improve on the quality of such a product so that by the time you improve on the product, your minimum star rating will be between three and five stars. Three is actually okay, since this is an average compared to one- or two-star rating.

This means you have to look for sellers in the top five with less than 50-100 reviews with poor quality listings. You need to create a superb listing, sell quality products and get good reviews. What makes a high quality listing is your title, high quality images, good descriptions with bullet points and a well written product description. You can actually jump anyone in ranking that has a poorer quality listing than yourself with less than 50-110 reviews.

If you use this rule of thumb, you can get into the top five listings. Making small changes to an item is certainly not necessary for your first product. It is icing on the cake if you can find a product that needs a simple tweak to make it perfect. The only way you will know if an item needs to be perfected is to read the existing reviews on Amazon. If it has a bunch of two-star reviews revealing that they love the item, but that something about the item is not good enough e.g. that a strap is not thick enough, you have hit the jackpot, since this is what you will have to discuss with your manufacturer on how to make the straps thicker and better.

Get factory pricing

Now that you have completed research and you have listed in your spreadsheet, that has the possible products to make sales in a short period of time with good reviews, you need to look for manufacturers, suppliers, wholesalers who are ready to private label for you. Once you have your preferred suppliers, the work is half done as you will only let them know the defects you have noticed in the product and what they can do to improve on its quality.

As a summary, here is a snapshot of the basic criteria that you need as a new seller to guarantee your success within a short period of time:

- Choose item priced between £10 - £40
- Must be lightweight and small (not more than 2kg)
- Sells 10 per day or more

- Sourced at most 25% of selling price (to give room for at least 30 - 45% profit)
- Must be under 500 reviews.

Steps to Good Sourcing

To ensure your success in getting the best product to sell and contacting manufacturers, you will need to ensure you take the following steps:

- Research the relevant category you wish to be selling on amazon by looking at the top 100 bestsellers. Read the reviews and come up with what you can do to make your own product stand out.
- Google search - this is very important as it is the only way you can get the list of suitable manufacturers.
- Qualification - this means you have to access very well the sites you have penciled down and pick only those you believe will be able to make a good quality product within the shortest period of time.
- Contact your shortlist - you will need to contact your suppliers in order to get started.
- Interview - you will have to interview your suppliers in order to ascertain whether they are right for you or not.
- Make your decision - this is the final stage at which you will have to use your gut instinct whether it is worth using the suppliers or not.

Steps to Amazon product research formula

To succeed in your search criteria, you will need to be able to:

- Identify keyword search volume
- Analyze top three amazon search results
- Analyze sales of your closest competitor
- Check current market trend using search engines
- Check supplier pricing

To help you achieve the above, I have listed below some of the tools that you need to do your product research.

Product Research

Google trends

Google trend is a public web tool based on searches that show how often a particular search term is entered relative to the total search volume across various regions of the world and in various languages. When you search for a term on trend, you will see a graph showing the term's popularity over a period of time - in real time. Just hover your mouse over the graph to examine different points on the graph and letters on the graph indicate news articles that might reveal why a certain term is spiking during that period of time.

To read and interpret the graph, hover your mouse over the graph. The numbers that appear show searches for a term relative to the total number of searches done on Google over time. Where there is a line trending downwards, this means that the term's search popularity is decreasing while upwards indicates the opposite. A downward trend does not mean that the total number of searches for that term is decreasing, it simply means it's popularity is decreasing compared to other searches.

Above the graph is a forecast checkbox. If you check the box, you will see a prediction of how popular the term will be in the near future. Google trend is a marketing insight and analysis tool that shows marketers the search volume of words and phrases over a select period of time and thus is a google marketing tools for anyone who wants to be a serious seller on amazon.

Google Keyword Tool

The Google keyword tool also enables you identify relevant keywords that people uses when searching for a particular item. The tool can be used to spy and swipe your competitor's keywords, you will also be able to find local keywords faster. It is also a wonderful tool for people looking for a specific niche markets or categories. To use the keyword tool, you must have a Gmail account and you will have to sign up for Google "adwords" account.

Camelcamelcamel

Camelcamelcamel is an Amazon price tracker that provides price drop alerts and price history charts for products that is being sold on Amazon. Some of its features are:

- Price drop and availability alerts
- Price history charts
- Amazon product search
- Wishlist import
- Twitter notifications

To learn more, please check http://camelcamelcamel.com/ as another free resource tool like the Google trends as well as their keyword tool.

Merchant words

Merchant words is a tracking tool for Amazon's keyword search as used by Amazon shoppers. The features are: Real Amazon Searches (which relate to the actual keyword that buyers use while shopping on Amazon); Search Volume (which shows the most popular search terms and the least popular searches); Unique Keyword data. This is not a free service and for example, Merchant words costs $30 per month for pro users, while it costs $900/month for enterprise accounts. You can learn more at https://www.merchantwords.com/.

Simple Keyword Inspector

This tool allows you to scrape and spy on competitors to see what keywords elevate their ranking. This can real help you to create new Pay Per Click (PPC) campaigns to help rank for your competitors keywords. Check It out on http://www.keywordinspector.com/.

AMZ Shark

This tool is great whether you are sourcing for a new product or spying on a competitor, as it provides you with real daily sales and re-stock figures for any product. It also allows to find hot new markets waiting to be exploited. If you wish to check it out, here is the link https://amzshark.com/.

Jungle Scout

Jungle Scout integrates into your Google Chrome browser, streamlining your product research. It extracts rank, sales volume, estimated revenue and more without ever exiting your browser or entering an Amazon product page. In addition, it displays number of reviews for a particular period, the seller who won Amazon buy box and you can also export the report into a csv file. If you are interested, here is the site: http://www.junglescout.com.

Selecting a Selling Plan

As I have mentioned above, you will need to decide if you want to be registered as an individual or a professional seller. If you plan to sell more than 40 items per month, your best bet will be to sign up as a professional seller; otherwise, if your items per month will be lower than 40, you should consider the individual plan. Selling in the professional category also enables you to add a new product that is not already on the Amazon marketplace or is already there but you want to be selling with your own brand (private label products). Note however, that you cannot sell "private label" under individual category.
The best option is to start as an individual seller with a limited product offering before registering as a professional seller as you will need to pay a monthly fee of £28.75 + VAT.

Selling on Amazon (Getting Started)

Selling on Amazon is as simple as 1, 2, 3, as all you have to do is to login to any of Amazon's website in which you are interested in selling from. I have already included the number of countries in which Amazon currently sells - all you have to do is decide in which of the countries you want to be registered. See below the links to each of the countries to assist you.

US - http://www.Amazon.com

UK - http://www.amazon.co.uk
France - http://www.amazon.fr
Spain - http://www.amazon.es
Italy - http://www.amazon.it
Germany - http://www.amazon.de
Japan - http://www.amazon.co.jp
China - http://www.amazon.cn
Australia - http://www.Amazon.au/
Brazil- http://www.Amazon.br/
Canada - http://www.amazon.ca/
India - http://www.amazon.in/
Mexico - http://www.Amazon.mx/
Netherlands - http://www.amazon.nl/

To be registered as a seller, you will need to login to any of the sites that you want to be selling, for instance, www.amazon.co.uk (I have decided to choose amazon UK as I reside in the United Kingdom and this is where I'm currently selling). When you login, scroll to the bottom of the page where you will see:

Click on "Sell on Amazon" and it will take you to this link: http://services.amazon.co.uk/services/sell-online/how-it-works-pro.html?ld=AZUKSOAFooterT1.

From here, you can read more about how it works, terms and conditions and more. Once, you have read about the terms and conditions, all you have to do is in three phases.

Register and set up your account

After you have selected the plan that you want, you will need to follow the step-by-step instructions to get your account up and running quickly. Be prepared to enter other information such as bank account details, address and other personal (or business) information.

Listing your products on Amazon is easy as you can basically just type in the model number of whatever you are trying to sell, or the ISBN number if it is a book, or a description, set the price you want to sell it for, and wait for buyers to start making purchases of your items. Unlike, eBay, there is no auction style option with Amazon. In addition, you don't have to take a picture of the item. Just describe your item accurately, name your price, watch and wait for sales to roll in.

Cost

A basic membership (individual plan) is free as mentioned earlier, however, an upgrade to professional costs £28.75/month plus VAT. The upgrade to professional will enable you to sell an item that is not already listed on the marketplace, or one that is private labeled. One nice feature of selling on Amazon is that you do not pay listing fee, - you only pay the Amazon fees when your item sells and if it does not sell, you pay nothing. You can read about Amazon's fees on their respective sites.

Getting Paid

When an item does sell, you are alerted by email depending on whether you are selling under merchant fulfilled (individual). If it is merchant fulfilled, the email will read something like; "Sold, dispatch now", while for "Fulfillment by Amazon" (FBA), the email will be like "Amazon.co.uk has dispatched the item you sold." I will explain more later about merchant vs Amazon fulfilled in later chapters.

You get paid 14 days after your item has been sold; however, for merchant fulfilled, you may have to wait a little longer. Amazon usually institutes at least a two week hold for your money, so if you need the money fast, Amazon may not be the way to go, you may wish to try out eBay where you have access to your funds immediately. Furthermore, if you are new seller, Amazon might reserve some of your funds for some time before releasing it to you. This is normal as they just want to know that you are good seller with ethical selling standards.

Pricing

With Amazon, you can see what all listed prices offered by other sellers and you can use other sellers' price to determine the price at which you sell your item.

Item Condition

Regarding the condition of your item, Amazon is better suited for items that are closer to "brand new" or "like new" as the buying clientele is more prone to buy brand new items rather than used items as it is on eBay.

Sources for Products to Sell

There are two main methods for sourcing items to sell on Amazon - reseller and private labels. If you are a beginner and you want other lower sources of sourcing for products, it will do you good to look at my Kindle book titled "Find It, Flip on Amazon".

Reseller

Reseller is a business model whereby an individual buys goods or products from wholesalers, suppliers and manufacturers with a plan to resell to potential buyers. After researching a product that sells well on either Amazon, eBay or other online marketplaces, an individual buys the item in bulk to resell to buyers with a profit margin.

If you want to be a reseller, you can either source your products domestically or internationally. Just login to Google, type in your desired keyword and add wholesalers, suppliers and manufacturers. You will see thousands of suppliers who make the product. Write down their details such as the site address, telephone number, email and give them a call to find out about pricing, shipping, tax and other details like the time it takes to deliver merchandise to you.

Follow up the phone call with an email to confirm your telephone discussion. This applies to international sourcing as well as domestic production, the only difference being that you have to read all about how to buy from international countries into your domicile country as it relates to tax, quality, the type of goods that is allowed into the country, rules and regulations of both countries.

If you have done your research well, you will have found the items that are hot selling. Order a few samples just to get started and once you are successful, you can order more quantities. Also, if you play your cards well, you can sell this particular item with decent profit for a very long time, even with many competitors.

The disadvantage with reseller though is that once it is discovered by other sellers that this item sells very well, you will soon see many sellers entering the same field with you and you can actually see a reduction in profit as those sellers will be prepared to sell at a lower price than you are or your profits disappearing completely.

Here are some sites to find products to sell under "reselling."

Ali Express - This website is like eBay, but only for sourcing products. The site makes it really easy to look for products and to get started with small order to start with before investing large amounts of money. The site's url is http://www.aliexpress.com.

Alibaba - Alibaba is the bigger fashion of Aliexpress where you can connect with suppliers, agents and manufacturers however on a larger scale. The minimum order quantity is sometimes enormous but with great pricing that will certainly help you to fight off competition. If you are starting small, I will advise you stick with Aliexpress. Alibaba's url is http://www.alibaba.com.

ThomasNet - is another site where you can connect with suppliers and manufacturers.

Globalsources - This is another very good site where you can source for a great number of hot selling products depending on the niche in which you want to trade in and it ranges from ranges health, beauty, electronics, fashions, bags, baby, the list is endless and the site is http://www.globalsources.com/.

Globalmarket - Another beautiful place to source for products and where you can also discuss/chat with suppliers so that they can understand your requirements better. The site is http://www.globalmarket.com/.

There are many other suppliers/manufacturers out there in the US, UK, China and more. Just Google research by typing keywords like private label manufacturers, suppliers, etc. and you can then streamline those you like after you might have visited the sites.

I use some of the tools that I have listed above, but not all of them. There are other tools out there which you can research on google, but to be honest with you, I only stick to the ones I have listed here and I'm just happy with the results achieved so far.

Private Label

In a nutshell, private label refers to products sold by one company under their own name but created/produced by another company. They cover a wide range of consumer goods such as electronics, health, beauty items and more. For you, private labelling will mean finding a specific hot-in-demand product, finding a supplier for that product and selling it as your own with your logo and branding. This means the smaller retailer places their own private brand label on the final good which was created by a third party manufacturer. Thus, private branding is a cost effective way to gain access to producing a product without requiring a large manufacturing or a design team.

The advantage of using private label for a specific product is that as a seller it gives you the edge over other sellers since this brand is your own and thus you do not face any competition from other sellers as nobody can copy your product (considered infringement of copyright). If any seller copies what you sell, you can sue and claim damages.

As a seller on Amazon, if you are thinking of making selling a long time or on a permanent basis, the option of private labelling is the best. Once you get it right, you can sell over and over again with decent profits each time you make sales. Just like in reseller, if you have done your research well, all you have to do is to look for manufacturers, suppliers of the product that you want to private label and contact the respective manufacturers so as to negotiate pricing, minimum order quantity (MQO), shipping and the rest.

To ensure you get your desired results, just type into google your keyword + private label and that returns a lot of results within few minutes. You will need to quickly assess the sites from the results that seem relevant to you and add them to your list. The only way you can achieve this is to open a spreadsheet, copy the manufacturer's website and contact details that you can refer to later after your initial research.

You may have to adjust your keyword by using terms like manufacturers, suppliers plus your keyword as most of these companies may not have included the word private label in their write up and if you don't do this, you might actually miss out on a good number of suppliers who are actually ready to allow you private label their products. Using all these phrases will guarantee you get the best suppliers that you can start to try to negotiate best prices and best products.

Once you have done your research, you will then need to qualify your list. This means checking each site more closely and eliminating the ones that do not seem right or suitable to you. After you have streamlined the potential manufacturers, note down their URL, email and telephone numbers including contact names.

You will then have to contact your shortlist of manufacturers. It is advisable to start with a telephone discussion after which you will follow with an email referring to your telephone conversation. This not a hard and fast rule though, as you might do the opposite which means sending email first and follow up with a telephone, just decide on which option is best for you. At other times, you might simply just want to ask for their Skype ID and chat with them via Skype.

Be prepared to ask your manufacturer a lot of questions such as manufacturing capacities, minimum order quantity, pricing, shipping, whether they sell the product themselves either online or via their own online store, whether they will do artwork/label or you have to look for a designer to do this for you. Also important is to ask for their lead time, which shows how long it takes to manufacture the product and how many days they require an advance notice to place stock replenishment.

It would be too much to list all the questions and other things you are expected as a beginner to ask your suppliers in this short book, hence, if you really want to become a pro on selling on amazon, please subscribe to my newsletter on my blog http://www.thesources.co.uk where you can learn more. Getting started with private labelling can be hard for most people and it was really one of the challenges that I had when starting out, but if you follow my advice and guidelines, this should be easy for you.

Getting your product to customers - delivery

Merchant versus fulfilment by Amazon "FBA"

You will need to decide how to deliver products - dispatch the goods yourself which is known as merchant fulfilled or to use Amazon in a program called "Fulfillment by Amazon" (FBA), as I have referred to earlier.

When you are a Merchant seller, after successfully uploading your inventory list, you will be responsible to ship the item to the buyer when it sells. This is where you get an email from Amazon like "Sold, dispatch now". FBA is a process whereby you ship all your items to be sold to one of the fulfillment centers and they will take over from there. This saves you time from having to manually manage your product inventory and ship out each individual product as it is being sold. You ship all your products to one of Amazon's designated facilities and they will take it up from there as they will handle the fulfillment of your products for you (packing, handling and shipping). In addition, you won't have to worry about storage space or going to the post office each time a sale is made, which to me is a huge time saver. One other major primary advantage of using FBA is that all Amazon Prime customers will be able to receive free shipping on any products they order from you.

FBA allows you to sell more and globally too, as you leave everything in the hands of Amazon. One major advantage of FBA over merchant selling is that you ship all your items once to the center for Amazon to handle.

To some, FBA is too expensive, but when you try it out, you will discover that though your margins might be small it can increase the number of items that customers buy from you. This is because Amazon is a household name and most buyers trust them more than individual sellers. At other times, you might decide to sell your items at a higher price than a merchant seller and it will surprise you that you get to sell your item first before a merchant does.

Buyers believe that FBA items are as good as the items that Amazon itself sells, since the item is in the custody of Amazon. Also, buyers are of the opinion that Amazon will never accept sub-standard items into its fulfillment centers, which in this case is true. Using the FBA system is usually better suited to any seller whether newbie or experienced seller. Just read about how it works and the applicable fees to enable you to understand it. To read about FBA, check the Amazon UK site:
http://services.Amazon.co.uk/services/fulfilment-by-Amazon/features-benefits.html.

The FBA unfair advantage

- Selling at prices way above non-FBA sellers
- Instant approvals to sell in categories non-FBA sellers have to apply for
- Access to an instant customer base of Amazon Prime customers, many of whom will never purchase non-FBA offers.
- Access to customers who use Amazon's free "Super Saver Shipping" option for which only FBA offers qualify
- Outsourced shipping - Amazon does it for you, as you only ship once to the FBA centre
- Outsource customer service - Amazon has taken this over from you.
- You can use FBA to fulfil your customers' orders on other channels like eBay your website and more.
- Leveraging the trust Amazon has built with internet consumers for more than 20 years. Although it is your product, customers know Amazon is doing the important work: shipping, packaging and providing coverage under Amazon's customer service policies.

- Effectively doubling your customer base as most buyers buying from you will not ordinarily buy from a merchant seller.

In addition to the above points, Amazon has already built the trust through their famed customer service reputation and we, as resellers or private label, just get to take advantage of all of it. Of course, they get a somewhat larger cut of the sales price, and though you might say, Amazon fee is high, it can substantially increase your sales.

There is really no significant downside. Most sellers' reaction includes the thought that extra fees are a pretty big downside, but they are actually not. Those fees are usually more than offset by the higher price you can sell for having that "Fulfilled by Amazon" logo next to your products.

FBA influence on your business

Fulfillment by Amazon is one of the best methods to keep your cost and time effective and increase your sales. With FBA, Amazon is your consignment center. You send your goods to them and they sell them on your behalf. There is no need to worry about shipping on time as Amazon sends your customer's order within 48 hours. As I have said, you will see by your listing - Fulfilled by Amazon with the word "Prime" in one of the corners.

What Prime means is that it is a paid service that gives amazon shoppers a few distinct advantages. Members of amazon prime are eligible for free two-day shipping on any item, without a minimum order balance as free shipping requires a minimum purchase of £20 in UK, while in the USA, it is $49. You can see using FBA can help you tap into the amazon prime members.

If a customer orders directly from Amazon, your product will get sent out automatically. In rare cases of refund requests, Amazon handles those, too. What is more amusing, if you get an order on eBay (assuming you sell on eBay too), your own website or anywhere else, just fill in the order details on Amazon and they will send it for you, from your FBA inventory, what is more you are only paying the cost of picking, packing - which you might have passed down to your eBay buyers. For order like this from other channels, Amazon does not get to be paid commission since the item was not sold on their site. It is as simple as A, B, C.

How to make your listing stand out

If you really want to make it on Amazon, you need to take extra care at ensuring that you take all the steps required to make your listing stand out from those of competitors. There are a lot of sellers on Amazon, but only those that are ready to take the bull by the horn actually make great and fantastic sales. It is only through your images, descriptions, etc that a buyer will make a decision whether he/she wants to buy the item from you. To ensure your listing stands out, you must do the following:

Your title

Title plays a key/major role in getting buyers attention to your listing. Your product title is the very first piece of information that a buyer will see when browsing, so you must make sure your titles are as specific as possible and using keywords that a buyer will ordinarily type into Amazon search engine to search for the products they are looking for.

Amazon allow 250 characters, but do yourself a favour and use only 100 characters (Amazon actually loves short titles). Include as many relevant keywords as possible by putting yourself in the position of the buyer when creating your titles, by considering what search terms you would use when shopping online. Buyers do not use words or punctuations such as gorgeous, flashy, caps or asterisks to search for items, so including any of these in your titles is a waste of time and valuable space.

Optimizing your product title for Amazon is an excellent way of ensuring that your product is presented to customers that searches for your product based on the keyword that the potential customers has typed into Amazon search engine box. This means that Amazon cares about keyword and this will do you good by cramming as many keywords that potential buyers will likely type into the search engine box.

Key product features and benefits

In describing your products features and benefits, you need to use bullet points that will highlight both the features and benefits of the product. It is not enough that your potential customers see your product. You must also be able to convince them that your product is the right choice. Bullets are the most visible and important text on your page aside from the title and if you mess this up could result in the buyers' turning elsewhere after all there are other sellers of the same product on Amazon.

Make sure you aim to sell your product to the page viewer from your bullet points by ensuring you use all of the bullet point areas. Use capital letters for the first few "main" words of each bullet point as these are your headlines. Ensure you repeat your keyword phrases in the bullet points though you may already have them in the title, there is no harm in repeating it in your bullet points - just capture the attention of buyers in both your titles and bullet points.

As a seller, you must make use of features/bullet points in order to convert lookers into "active buyers". Features which are displayed as bullet points that is right below the pricing and product options, is an absolute must. See below a good example of proper feature usage and I'm sure you will want to adopt the format into your own listing, too, in order to attract great buyers:

Roll over image to zoom in

Fire, 7" Display, Wi-Fi, 8 GB - Includes Special Offers, Black
by Amazon

#1 Best Seller in Computers & Accessories

Price $49.99 & FREE Shipping. Details

Select options after adding to cart

This item will be released on September 30, 2015
Pre-order now.
Ships from and sold by Amazon.com. Gift-wrap available.

Due to popular demand, new Fire orders may ship later than **September 30th, 2015**

- Beautiful 7" IPS display (171 ppi / 1024 x 600) and fast 1.3 GHz quad-core processor. Rear and front-facing cameras
- All-new Amazon Underground, a one-of-a-kind app store experience where over $10,000 in apps, games and even in-app items are actually free - including extra lives, unlocked levels, unlimited add-on packs and more
- Enjoy more than 38 million movies, TV shows, songs, books, apps and games
- 8 GB of internal storage. Free unlimited cloud storage for all Amazon content and photos taken with Fire devices. Add a microSD card for up to 128 GB of additional storage
- Updated user Interface - Fire OS 5 designed for quick access to your apps and content plus personalized recommendations that make it easy to discover new favorites
- Up to 7 hours of reading, surfing the web, watching videos, and listening to music
- Stay connected with fast web browsing, email, and calendar support

I'm sure you notice how the bullet points are extremely detailed and include several keywords that are easily readable. This means buyers will be able to find this item quicker than other sellers who have failed to capitalize on the use of features and bullet points.

A specification is the part of the page (shown below) where you actually list the technical and physical details of your product. This includes size, weight, storage, shipping weight, colours and other necessary information that will guide potential buyers into making a decision whether to buy or not. All these are necessary since there are millions of sellers all competing to sell the same products and it is only the sellers who took the necessary steps to list in a professional manner that gets the sales. See an example below:

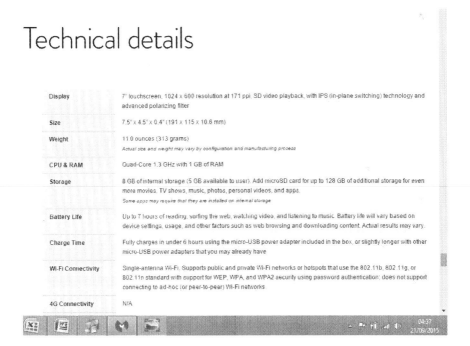

Technical details

Display	7" touchscreen, 1024 x 600 resolution at 171 ppi. SD video playback, with IPS (in-plane switching) technology and advanced polarizing filter
Size	7.5" x 4.5" x 0.4" (191 x 115 x 10.6 mm)
Weight	11.0 ounces (313 grams) *Actual size and weight may vary by configuration and manufacturing process*
CPU & RAM	Quad-Core 1.3 GHz with 1 GB of RAM
Storage	8 GB of internal storage (5 GB available to user). Add microSD card for up to 128 GB of additional storage for even more movies, TV shows, music, photos, personal videos, and apps. *Some apps may require that they are installed on internal storage*
Battery Life	Up to 7 hours of reading, surfing the web, watching video, and listening to music. Battery life will vary based on device settings, usage, and other factors such as web browsing and downloading content. Actual results may vary.
Charge Time	Fully charges in under 6 hours using the micro-USB power adapter included in the box, or slightly longer with other micro-USB power adapters that you may already have
Wi-Fi Connectivity	Single-antenna Wi-Fi. Supports public and private Wi-Fi networks or hotspots that use the 802.11b, 802.11g, or 802.11n standard with support for WEP, WPA, and WPA2 security using password authentication; does not support connecting to ad-hoc (or peer-to-peer) Wi-Fi networks
4G Connectivity	N/A

Product description

I have also mentioned the product description. This is part of what Amazon uses to put your products in front of its massive buyers, then write good product descriptions and expand on the features of the products. When I first

35

started on Amazon, I did not take all these into consideration as I have no idea or any hint that this is necessary to convert potential buyers into "actual buyers". However, once I understood and put them into practice, I began to get more sales and on some occasions have won the buy box. Take a look below at the product description of the above tablet:

The description may not be the first thing that the buyer will see; however, that is where the sale is made most of the time. At this point, your prospect is already intrigued and investing the time to learn more about your product. If you can give them more detailed information that they are looking for in the description and confirm that they are making the right choice with your product, you are going to make a sale. This means providing the most detailed product description can give you a better chance of tempting more customers. This can be a balancing act, as burdening buyers with too much information can also be off-putting.

To balance the two sides, keep your description to around 200 words including what you think are the most relevant selling points of your product. Some categories equally allow up to eight bullet points in the product descriptions, so use them to convey a high-level overview of the product with the broadest appeal. Adding a quality description and bullet points will contribute to increased conversion.

In addition, you must target the exact keyword strings you want to rank for in your description. Use the description to reiterate the primary benefits of your product, address the prospect's problem and present your product as the solution. Include clear product information which must include common uses, ingredients (if this is applicable), warranty information, guarantee and more. Also ensure you use every long tail keyword as much as possible. You have the space to use here, so take advantage of it to further lure away the buyers to your side.

Images

Amazon is very strict when it comes to image size and quality as it requires an image that is at least 1,000 x 1,000 pixels or even larger. The image taken must also be of a pure white background - any image out of these criteria will be suppressed. The 1,000 x 1,000 pixels image allows Amazon to offer customers their Hover-to-Zoom feature, which it believes has a dramatic effect on conversion rates (see the zoomed images of the above captioned tablet below and notice the dramatic effect it might have on potential buyers who will interestingly become real buyers as a result of this zoomed image.

Images are an essential part of listing as without good quality images, you may not be able to attract customers to your listing. It is true that images drive consumer confidence, and this is no longer just a nice addition, it is a requirement for success. According to a recent research from buyers, images improve the overall experience and confidence for customers as it is easier for

37

shoppers to find, evaluate and purchase products since they cannot see the product physically as in a street storefront.

Amazon is actually strict in its requirement that images must accurately represent the actual product for sale with minimal of no propping that can mislead consumers, in addition it must be at least 1,000 x 1,000 pixels. My advice is that you make it 1,000 x 1,000 pixels. Ensure you use attractive looking images and this is a must since if your product looks like junk, you will not get many sales. Invest in high quality images by using the service of a photographer or a freelancer site like fiverr (www.fiverr.com) (http://www.editmyphoto.co.uk/) to get good quality images for your products.

Amazon makes an allowance for nine images. Ensure you use at least seven to give the buyers a real time experience by exploring the images which will encourage them to buy from you.

Reviews

Amazon has pretty much trained online shoppers to read reviews prior to making a purchase. The more positive reviews you get, both for the product and as a seller, the better your chances of making a sale.

Higher conversion rates keep customers on your page and makes it more likely they will buy your products. Amazon ranks products with multiple options in their listing above those without multiple options.

On a humorous note, reviews have even been turned into viral content as in the case of the BIC Pen designed for women:

Amazon reports that only 10 to 20 percent of buyers leave feedback after their purchases and this is true. I have sold countless of items yet the feedback received are not that many. I have sent several emails to request for feedbacks which most buyers simply ignore. Can you blame them? No, they have made the purchase, happy with their products, so end of story. It is only when the item is not good or does not meet their expectations that you will receive negative feedback that if not addressed in a professional manner can dent your image. Since we can't compel buyers to leave feedback, here are some tips to increase your chances of success:

- If you sell via other channels as well, reach out to your existing base of satisfied customers and ask them to leave some product feedback.

- You can also do an outreach campaign via your social media channels to request product feedback.

- Amazon also allows you to provide a product for free if you ask for an unbiased honest review. They don't allow offering any incentives for a positive review or requesting a buyer to give you five-star rating so be careful how you phrase this.

- Request feedback via your seller account from buyers on Amazon, who can leave not only product feedback but also seller feedback. Though with all these, you may still not receive any feedback. However, you have tried so you need to move on.

Reduce your chances of receiving negative feedback/reviews by understanding the most common causes for buyers to complain:

- Product out of stock

- Item not as described (pay close attention to this, it can actually send you out as a seller from Amazon platform)

- Late shipments

- Incorrect item shipped

- Damaged in transit

- Complicated return process

Given how customer-centric Amazon is, shoppers have been conditioned to expect fast shipments and products that meet the quality guidelines. Any deviations from these high standards can cost you more than just negative feedback; processing a return or reshipment does cost some money too. Also, Amazon might actually suspend you or close your account totally.

Too many negative seller reviews can even have your account suspended, so be careful to always put the customer first, just as Amazon does. The better reviews will really pay off in your sales and profit in future.

How your products rank on Amazon – listing your products right

Amazon has a search engine algorithm known as the A9 Algorithm, which calculates three core variables when giving the customer results and these are:

1. Conversion rate – how many sales the link might bring which is based on history, customer reviews, price and more.

2. Relevancy – how similar the product is to the search term that the customer has entered which is based on title, description and keywords,

3. Customer satisfaction and retention – how often does customers' come back to buy based on feedback, order defect rate.

To be able to know this you will have to understand the metric used by Amazon which are:

Sales rank

The simplest way to know how good a product is doing in its category is by the number of sales compared to other similar products which is otherwise known as "Sales Rank" and this is one of the most important ranking factors. This has an attribute of conversation rate, which is associated to price. They look at the history of people clicking on your link and ending up as customers for this listing is pricing as customers tend to seek the best deals.

In-Stock rate

Amazon's two of its big customer satisfaction metrics are percentage of orders refunded and pre-fulfillment cancellation. In either case, Amazon has found that vendors/sellers with low in-stock rates tend to have higher refunds and cancellations, which is bad for customer retention. As a seller, I'm sure you will want to avoid falling into each of the above listed metrics.

Get buyers to your listing and captured them with good service so they will stay with you for a very long time, purchasing over and over again, which is turning first time buyers into repeat buyers.

Driving traffic and sales

Now that your product listing page is built, it is time to drive targeted traffic to generate sales. There are several ways of generating traffic to your listings, some of which are:

Search terms

Amazon has five fields that accept 50 characters each; hence you do not need to repeat any words. Commas will be ignored and quotation marks will unnecessarily limit your keyword. Including multiple variations of the same word is unnecessary and also including common misspelling is unnecessary, too. Order of search terms is relevant and also make sure you include synonyms or spelling variations e.g. sun cream and suncream, since most buyers will type it differently though they are searching for the same item.

Parent-child products

If you have a few variations of the same product (colours, sizes, etc.) it will be best to use Amazon's in-built parent-child product functionality to direct all customers to a single product page, rather than create multiple listings for variations of the same product. If you put all options into one listing, this will ensure potential buyers are able to find the related products on the same page.

Word of mouth

Your first customers should be friends and family members. Introduce your products to your friends and family members and request them to help spread the word among their colleagues. Give your family, friends the product free in order to give it a trial and see if the product is good as described. It is against Amazon terms of service (TOS) for friends and family to leave reviews, however, giving the product to them to use can give them the confidence to market your product to their colleagues and others. Make flyers for your item which you can and you should give to your family/friends to distribute as they assist you in marketing your product. To me, this is a good way to get word out about your item as it can actually drive traffic to your listing.

Social media

Social media is a great way of generating free traffic to your listing on Amazon. If you have a Facebook account, you can create a fan page where you can start to gather friends together by searching for people and groups to join or make friends. There are so many people or groups with the same interest on Facebook, just search and you will see them. Here's how to use each of the seven social media methods to promote your Amazon listings.

Facebook

Facebook is perhaps the single most powerful social media for friends, family, buyers, sellers, authors and more. You must have a fan page devoted to your items, you will also have to post the images of the items that you are selling into your Facebook fan page. Take advantage of fan pages - search for groups and fan pages devoted to your niche, especially for those that focus specifically on the items you have to sell. Make sure you check their rules and if they allow promotion, then do it.

Most groups allow members to ask for reviews for the products that they are selling either to give the item free or at a heavily discounted price for an unbiased/honest review of the product, utilize this if this is available in the groups that you join.

Pinterest

Pinterest is a growing social platform that mostly focuses on sharing images. You will need to create "pin boards" on which you pin various images. You can create separate boards for each of the items you are selling and ask people to re-pin your item in order to gain a wider audience with the possible clicking to your listing on Amazon which can result in a sale if they like what you have to offer. You can also share your pin and boards on Facebook, twitter and elsewhere in order to get as much exposure as possible to your items.

Instagram

Instagram is a very simple, easy to use, visual form of social media. This makes it perfect for any small business selling products that are interesting or easy to photograph. Engagement on Instagram is 15 times higher than on Facebook, take advantage of this to increase your brand awareness by looking for a community of followers that have the interest of what you are selling, who will also share an insight and behind the scenes peek into your business.

Twitter

Twitter is another great social platform if you use it properly. You can create a list of followers by looking for people or groups in your chosen niche. Make sure you tweet about your products, but do not bug people too often. If you are really active on twitter, you will discover that twitter management will start sending you great ideas on how to grow your followers, who to follow to get maximum exposure for your niche.

Linkedin

LinkedIn has great tools for connecting you with friends, colleagues, customers and prospects. The key to your success on LinkedIn is your profile. Make sure you take time to fill them out properly and use it to promote yourself. If you are able to do this well, you will get people who will like to be in your network. From there, you can start promoting your business.

Google Plus

With over 150 million active users, and more than 50% logging into Google plus daily, it is a social platform you can't ignore as it can help impact your search engine rankings in a positive way. You can use Google plus to leverage:

Authorship – this is a great way to get your picture next to your listings in the search results

Relationship marketing – with google hangouts, you can connect with and get to know your fans.

Driving traffic – by building up your google plus profile, you can share content and news about your business and it is a simple way of driving traffic to your business.

YouTube

YouTube is a great platform for promotion of anything. Just create a simple video to promote your items. If you cannot do this on your own, go to fiverr.com or upwork.com to look for video creation freelancers who are ready to do this for you at a minimal cost and will even post it to YouTube for you (if that is what you want). You can also post the video to the site by yourself. Once you upload your video to YouTube, don't forget to share it on Facebook, twitter, pin interest and others for maximum exposure.

Blogging

Blogging is a good way of generating targeted traffic to your Amazon listing. All you have to do is to have a domain site where you write a comprehensive report or interesting topics/subjects with a linking to your Amazon listings. You can then post to the social media sites or you can also buy a few advertising to promote your blogs. As reader read your posts on your blog, they might or will click on the listing link that takes them to your products on Amazon and might actually make purchases of your product.

You can also look for blogs that relates to your niche, sign up as guest blogger, add your signature (which will include your link to your listing on Amazon); always ensure you make a good contribution/suggestion as this will earn you good points that will make readers of such blogs click on your link which will ultimately take them to your listing and who knows, you might make some sales.

Free classified advertisements

Classified advertising is a free online advertising that allows you to advertise your services or products more especially to your local community. It is a short ad in a newspaper, magazine or online and appearing along with other ads of the same type. Most of these services are free and some may require a little fee to advertise for you. Some of the popular classified adverts are:

* Craigslist

* Gum Tree

* OLX.com

* Oodle

* Adpost

* Salespider.com

* Adlandpro

* USfreeads

And many more (search for it on Google)

Now that we have talked about free traffic, it is time to learn about paid traffic. Paid traffic is an inducer that can give you targeted buyers. In fact, without paid ads, you will not make great sales as free traffic might not bring you the expected sales surge.

Amazon Sponsored Products Ads

One great way to drive traffic back to your product listing page is what is known as Amazon Sponsored Products Ads, which are ads made by Amazon that can assist to drive traffic back to your product listing pages on Amazon. These ads show up alongside the search results for the keywords you choose and provide additional visibility for your products. Look at the example below:

More Colors Available	More Colors Available	More Colors Available	More Colors Available
New Balance Men's M750 Athletic Running Shoe	ASICS Men's GEL Contend Running Shoe	Saucony Women's Cohesion 6 Running Shoe	Reebok Men's Pheehan Running Shoe
$54.99 - $82.50 prime	$30.00 - $89.99 prime	$39.98 - $96.00 prime	$29.98 - $69.55 prime
Some selection are Prime eligible	Some selection are Prime eligible	Some selection are Prime eligible	Some selection are Prime eligible
★★★★☆ (79)	★★★★☆ (129)	★★★★☆ (55)	★★★★☆ (141)
Show only New Balance items	Show only ASICS items	Show only Saucony items	Show only Reebok items
Shoes: See all 21,337 items	Sports & Outdoors: See all 17,700 items	Shoes: See all 21,337 items	Sports & Outdoors: See all 17,700 items

Sponsored Products on Amazon (related)

Adidas Mens Climawarm Falcon Running Shoes 13 Us
$69.95
prime
Fashion Footwear

Salomon Women's Fellraiser W Trail Running Shoe,Black,6.5 M US
$109.95
★★★★☆ (3)
Backcountry

It is extremely easy to get started. There are no ads to write; all you do is select your keywords and your products and set the bids. Also, you might want to start with automatic ad campaigns, which is where you won't even need to choose/write any keywords or copy anything. Amazon does this simply based on the relevant keywords that customers looking for your products are typing into their search engine. With careful selection of keywords and targeting, the chances of a sale are extremely high since buyers on Amazon tend to have a higher intent to purchase, leading to less wasted clicks than with other Pay Per Click (PPC) programs.

There is another added benefit, too. The additional sales generated from this improve the page's sales rank, which in turn improves its rankings in the organic listings.

You will also do yourself a good advantage by making use of Google AdWords, Bing and Yahoo in addition to Facebook advertising. You will be able to target your ads on these sites to people who are looking for the products that you are selling on Amazon marketplace. These ads will generate traffic by putting links to your products in Google searches, Yahoo, Bing and Facebook. Once you are able to generate traffic that converts to sales, soon you will not need to spend money on advertising as you have succeeded in turning your buyers into repeat customers and also generating new buyers purely organic as a result of positive reviews. If you are new or even experienced but do not have the technicality to set up Google Adwords, Facebook, freelance services are available on sites like fiverr.com, upwork.com, freelancer.com and more if you can do the search on Google.

In addition to the above, make sure you offer good customer service. Treat people the way you want to be treated. Follow up with your customers after making a purchase by thanking them for their purchases and telling them to leave a feedback on their buying experience. Like I said earlier, most buyers will still not leave any feedback, however, it is good to always do this as you can turn that customer to a repeat customer. Having a positive, memorable interaction with your buyers will make customers want to buy from you again. Always provide promotions or offer other incentives to get buyers to continue to purchase from you (this is really possible via Facebook).
You can also entice customers by offering them additional items for free or the lowest price in addition to using buy one get the second half price or free as this tactic can work for you as an Amazon seller.

Getting reviews for your products

There are a few ways you can get reviews for your products without being dishonest or resorting to tactics that could get you banned by Amazon.

Facebook groups

The very first set of people that you can get reviews from are people that have become your friends via Facebook. Ask them to purchase your item (and if they are unwilling to do this because they do not want to spend money, give the product to them free) or at a heavily discounted price and then write an unbiased, honest review. Please do not tell them to give you five-star review, but leave them to test the product and give the review as it appeals to them.

Giveaways

With giveaways, you will have to look for people possibly on the social media or websites about the types of products you sell. Give them the product free in exchange for an unbiased review. There are also other reviewers on Amazon where you can do the same thing.

Bloggers

To get bloggers to review your product, you will have to find them by researching on Google, Bing, Yahoo or other search engines and this has to relate to the niche that you are selling into. Once you get them, offer the products free to them in exchange for an honest review of the item.

Coupon Codes

You can also buy coupon codes, typically a heavily discounted coupon code on popular sites like snagshout, (applicable only to Amazon US) (www.snagshout.com) to give to people who will use the coupon to purchase the item from Amazon and will leave a review in exchange for the discounted coupon codes. If you like the idea of giving coupon codes in exchange for a review, check this site where you will see tons of other coupon providers – http://vonbeau.com/offer/get-free-and-discounted-products-to-review-on-amazon.htm. If you are in the UK and you will be selling on Amazon UK, the site to get your coupon codes is https://www.ilovetoreview.com/

Growing your profits

As an Amazon seller, it is important to understand how to grow your profits by building the type of business you always wanted. If you have started out as "Merchant fulfilled" i.e. shipping the items to your buyers when it sells and you are now bugged down with these, do yourself a favour by switching to Fulfilment by Amazon (FBA). With FBA, all your items will be shipped once to an Amazon fulfilment centre where they will take over packing and shipping to customers that buys from you. If you truly follow my write-up on "The unfair advantage of FBA," you will by now understand that it is better to switch to FBA.

Furthermore, you will be able to free up your time to do other important things such as having more time to research products or watch your metrics in order to make more sales. More sales bring in more profits.

Acquire more inventories

One way to increase your profits is to add more products to your chosen category. Having new/more products in your chosen niche is one of the ways in which you can grow your business. If you stick to only one item, a time might come when this particular item might not be in hot demand as buyers' tastes/requirements changes overtime. It is thus wise to introduce new item as soon as you become successful in the first introduced item into the marketplace. This will also ensure you have many different items to offer to your buyers and you will continue to sell regardless of whatever is happening to a particular item. All you have to do is to study each of the categories/sub-categories and use this study to decide which ones you will add to your existing products where you are currently selling.

You will need to try a few items to see how it goes before buying more stock or private labelling the products. If it is successful, then move forward with larger bulk purchases or outright private label the products, as I'm now an advocate of making the items in your own brand to ward off competitors.

Be sure to outsource and automate your listings as one of the most time-consuming tasks you will have as an Amazon seller is the physical component of listing items for sale. There is software available to help you list items faster such as Inventory Loader, or you can hire a Virtual Assistant (freelance sites) to help with listing items. Many Virtual Assistants will enjoy listing items for you at very moderate charges, so that you can use your time for something else.

Higher sales

Online marketplaces are huge, in UK alone according to one analysis, there are more than 17.7 million unique visitors to eBay each month and an item is sold every second. And Amazon, the core of this book: it is the most visited website with more than 20 million unique visitors every month and with sales occurring every second of the day. This means when you sell in more than one marketplace, you will discover that you will sell more items in a day compared to the numbers that you will be selling in only one marketplace.

Shoppers go to their preferred marketplaces. While some shoppers are addicted to Amazon, others are to eBay, while others will go to other places like , Gum Tree, Buy.com, Volusion, and more. The potential to get your product in front of customers and lift up your sales volume is simply staggering. Marketplaces are where the buyers are in vast numbers.

Believe me, if you have your online store in most of these places you can sell more than 100 items in a day and I believe this is good for you as you will be able to achieve your dreams of working from home and have more time for yourself, family and loved ones. In addition, you make more money.

Watch your metrics

Keeping track of numbers is an important aspect of running any business, especially a retail business. If you are not sure what your costs are, and how much profit you are earning on each item, then you are not doing a good job. You must keep tabs on fees as well as what you pay for an item. Kindly consider how much it costs to run your business so that you can always price your items correctly and earn a decent profit.

Growing your profits takes thoughtful consideration of each part of your business such as buying, fulfilling orders, managing your time all play a factor of making your Amazon marketplace business a huge success. If you really want a big chunk of big profits, you must pay attention to this aspect of your business.

Customer service

You will remember that I have mentioned a lot about customer service. You cannot afford to toy with this as it can cause you a great disservice if you neglect it. If you use FBA, Amazon will hand your customer service for you such that if something went wrong with the item, Amazon will take the item back, refund the money, and properly debit or credit your account for you.

You will still need to deal with some common issues such as following up with the buyer to explain what has happened and how you intend to avert such situation in future.

In some cases, (though rare) where a customer has left you with a one-star rating, you will have to extend an olive branch, where you will possibly replace the item to ensure the negative feedback is deleted by the buyer as this can seriously impact your business - who wants to really make a purchase from a seller with one-star rating feedback? No one and I'm sure you will not want to buy from such a seller either.

On the other hand, if you register as an individual merchant, whereby you are the one that packed and shipped the items, you will have to do the customer service yourself and still need to explain to the buyer what has happened.

Customer reviews

Keep a close watch on customer feedback, as feedbacks can literally kill your business if it is negative and you do nothing about it. You may have to deal with buyer's remorse, or an actual problem with your product mentioned within a customer review. When you read the reviews, ask yourself if the customer has a point, and if it does, reach out to the customer to offer a replacement, a refund, etc. Doing it this way, will ensure such negative reviews are removed by the buyers and will even give such buyers more confidence to buy from you in future (repeat customer right?).
However, if the buyer is just being nasty as it can happen, you can actually reach out to Amazon and request for certain negative comments to be removed if:

- The feedback includes foul language
- The feedback was a product review
- The feedback was a complaint about order fulfilment where FBA is used

Typically, if Amazon agrees with you, the bad review will be removed within 24 to 48 hours. You will need to contact Amazon via your Amazon Seller Central Dashboard.

Common mistakes to avoid

As in most business models, there have been plenty of people who have tried it before you and failed all because they were not patient enough or made mistakes which they have simply refused to correct and thereby gave up. When it comes to selling online more especially in the marketplaces, you will have to learn, be patient, look at what others are doing that make them successful, copy some of their ideas and you will be a success. It is important that you try not to reinvent the wheel, just learn from people who have done it and succeeded.

Listed below are some common mistakes that new sellers make so that you can try to avoid them.

Not spending money

The amount of money you invested in your business is proportionate to how much you expect to earn in your business. If you only put up 10 low-cost inventory products, you cannot expect to make six or seven figures income per year. If you need to make that much, you need to invest proportionate amount to meet your expectations. This means that when you want to buy merchandise, you must find out if those items are selling well, know the retail value, and calculate the profit that you will make from selling the items, also your branding must be unique. If you want to make six figures income, the retail value must be in the region of seven to eight to give room for exigencies that may arise.

Furthermore, you will have to spend tangible amount on advertising to get your product in front of hungry buyers. You will have to use Amazon sponsored product ads, Google AdWords, Facebook and more. These advertisements will pay for themselves over and over once your products are discovered by buyers. A time will come when you will no longer need paid advertising as you will now be getting quality organic traffic which is free - how sweet can that be.

Not placing value on time

A lot of new business owners do not place any value on their time. This is understandable because most business owners work for free for a lot of hours before turning a profit. People who do not understand their own value will often forgo the idea of using fulfillment services because they think the fees are too high. But if you think carefully, you will know that your time is worth more as you have little hours in the day to invest in your business.

When you outsource or use fulfillment services, you have more time to devote to other issues which can also bring you more profit as you will have time to think on what other investment you can incorporate with your selling. With strategic outsourcing, you can make the most of your time while increasing your profit potential; you will also have time to look after your life and that of your family.

Starting without a clear plan

Every business owner needs to start their business with a plan that includes both the vision and mission statement - business plans are not only for corporations but for individuals as well. If you fail to plan, you have planned to fail. A business plan is essential to your success. This will help you determine what type of products you want to sell, the categories of people you want to sell to, how you will price your items, your branding, how many products you need to sell to earn the kind of money you will like to make. Without these in place, you are just starting another hobby which can die off easily. With a plan, you are starting a real business with real profit potential and lasting lifetime.

Pricing items incorrectly

If you price your items too low, you will lose money and if your price also is too high, you will lose money as you will not get too many buyers. You have to balance these two in order to stay profitable. Study your competitors to know the right price to pick and look for ways of beating them hands down by studying the trends in the market.

Let me tell you that the worst offender is pricing products too low as you make a sale you think you are successful, but once you reconcile your books you will realize that you have actually lost money. I'm sure you do not want this. So, you have to keep in mind selling fees, per order fees, shipping costs and other costs associated to your items which can affect your profit potentials.

Describing items inaccurately

Amazon has a feature that allows you to enter a UPC code of an item, or an ISBN number for books to automatically list an item without having to put in a separate description of each item. You will want to use this feature; however, you need to check it to be certain that it is right for you. Sometimes, data entry errors happen but other times the number has changed and it brings up a different product entirely. This can be a customer service nightmare and can affect your seller rating negatively, so you must pay close attention.

In other cases, too as a seller, you might want to borrow a keyword to include in your title which in your attempt to bring in buyers and make sales is not actually what the item says. This is dangerous, do not attempt to include keyword that is not associated with your item, this will backfire as buyers will return this item back to you and leave a very bad feedback which I'm sure you do not want. Negative feedback will kill your business at an alarming rate, so try to avoid it as much as you can.

Mismanaging inventory

If you choose to sell items at more than one marketplace, it is essential that you keep track of your inventory all the time. If you are only selling in one marketplace like Amazon and using FBA, it will be easier to keep track of your inventory. However, if you sell in more than one marketplaces, you will have to keep track of your inventory so that you will not be apologizing to buyers most of the time that you are out of stock without knowing.

A good way to do this, is to allocate a set number to each outlet, such as 20 items for Amazon, 15 for eBay and so forth. Doing it this way will ensure that you won't have to disappoint someone who ordered from you because you did not realize you were out of stock. They are also so many accounting software that you will like to buy once you become established as you will not like to spend too much money getting started when you are relatively new in the business.

Not following Amazon guidelines

Amazon has a long list of rules and guidelines; you need to read them; get to know them and also have it at the back of your hand so that you do not violate any of the rules. If you do, Amazon will suspend your account in a jiffy whisker. Each relevant category has acceptable terms and rules for listing items for instance, used games must be listed as collector's items and not used games for the listing to be accepted. Make sure you read the guidelines for the category you want to be selling in before you start purchasing items to sell in that category so that you are aware from day one what is acceptable and not acceptable.

Failing to connect with buyers

If you use Amazon FBA, there is no way you can add flyers or business card when your item is dispatched. However, there is a way round it as Amazon allow you to send email to your buyers to connect with them from your seller central account. Use this to welcome them into your store and thanking them very much for purchasing from you. Amazon displays buyers name and address - make sure you copy this details into a worksheet as you can always send them flyers to introduce new items you have to sell or even introducing them to your other online marketplaces or even your own e-commerce store.

Any opportunity you have to interact with your buyers is for the better. Try as much as possible to avoid the mistakes that have already been made by those sellers who were there before you. In this business, to really succeed within a short period of time, you need a mentor or a coach who has experience creating successful Amazon business.

If you like I can be your mentor/coach and you will see how you can connect with me at the end of this book. I'm also starting a membership site where you will be able to learn more about selling on the internet. If I can do it successfully, you too can.

Not handling customers' complaints on time

As a seller, you will on some occasions, receive customer complaints. Just like in customer reviews, you will have to deal with the complaints as soon as possible and in a professional manner. How far you deal with a customer complaint will affect your seller rating dramatically; therefore, deal with the issue immediately giving the customer the benefits of the doubt. While it is a popular opinion that customers are always right, there are situations when they are not.

However, you must weigh how important being right is when you want to keep your seller rating high, and you want to rid yourself of the problem. Sometimes, you might have to take the insult and make things right with the buyer, even though you have done nothing wrong. To avoid complaints, make sure you provide very accurate product titles as many complaints come because the item received did not match the description in the buyer's mind.

Be specific in your descriptions by giving full details of the item including the images. If it is an item that is used but like new, state this in your title/descriptions to avoid complaints. Always "under promise but over deliver" so the buyer will be thrilled and will continue to buy from you when you have items that the buyer is interested in.

Customer service is about building relationships with your buyers by answering them quickly and dealing with issues right away, you will create a trusting relationship and the customers are sure to want to buy from you again. Please take to the advice as I'm talking to you from my own experience.

Putting everything together

It is possible to make six or seven figures income by selling on the Amazon marketplace and others if you plan your business right. You can work for yourself doing something that is completely legitimate, making more profit than you think is possible, all from the comfort of your home, or if you prefer, using an office. Some categories require approval to sell on Amazon, called

"Gated categories." When you sign up to become a seller, you will be able to read all about it. If you do it right the way it should be done, you will be approved for those gated categories.

The Amazon Marketplace offers tremendous opportunity to a business owner ready to take their sales to a whole new level. They have all the help you could need available through their FBA services and more. Thousands of people per day are searching for merchandise through the marketplace, giving you an unprecedented chance to reach your market without the massive marketing expense typically necessary to grow a business to this level.

While there is a tremendous amount of information to learn about starting or expanding a current business with the Amazon Marketplace, the resources are out there to help you get started right so that you can work toward unleashing big profits.

Sell in other marketplaces

Once you become an established seller on Amazon, to truly make a six figure sales, you will have to add other marketplaces to establish your presence. If you want to make money that will enable you to work from home by firing your boss, you have to sell in multiple places so that you can sell more. On Amazon alone, you can sell in more than five marketplaces in both Europe and USA (as you are not restricted to one marketplace). Furthermore, you can also sell on eBay platform as eBay also has so many marketplaces. There are many reasons/advantages for selling in online marketplaces which I have listed below:

Lower risk

If you only sell through one channel, what happens when something goes wrong? If you rely on advertising like Google Adwords, Bing or Yahoo, new competitors could push costs up so high that they are no longer affordable. Let's assume that your buyers favour a limited range of products, and your wholesaler puts their prices up for those products, or can no longer source them, then your profits could plummet.

Marketplaces offer an easy way to diversify – there will always be risks – marketplaces have plenty of them too – but if each of your sales channels have slightly different risks, you will have a good degree of protection against the many unpredictable problems that can happen in business.

Scale and efficiency

When you sell more, and become a bigger business, new opportunities will open up. Selling on marketplaces can provide a way to get that larger sales volume, and help grow a bigger business. Then you could buy larger quantities of stock, get better prices from suppliers, and increase your profit margin. It is possible to hire people to specialize in specific areas like marketing or logistics. If your business gets better at marketing, sales will grow further. If you get more efficient at handling stock and fulfilling orders, costs will fall. A larger scale of business can open up new sourcing opportunities too and brand names may be willing to sell to you.

Marketing

Selling on marketplaces may seem to work against developing your own brand, but this does not have to be that way. The larger scale of trade means there are more opportunities to be seen by customers. For instance, on eBay, there is a lot of freedom to design your store and products pages however you like, so buyers get a real feel for who they are buying from. There is much less freedom on Amazon, but you can still include a discount flier in the item you send to buyers (more especially if it is Merchant fulfilled) to motivate the customer to buy next time. This depends on what you are selling; if your products appeal to an enthusiastic audience, such as those with a niche hobby or pastime, there is a lot of potential to make yourself known to them through the marketplaces, then drive repeat sales through your own store.

Cross-border trade

Cross-border trade (CBT) is where you make direct sales to overseas buyers. The big global marketplaces – Amazon has made a big deal out of CBT even with eBay. The two marketplaces have put a lot of effort into making it easy to trade this way, with services to help with translation, listing, postage, returns and more. Amazon has marketplaces in five EU countries as I have highlighted earlier in addition to US, Canada, Japan, China and India, while eBay has presence in about 26 countries.

Selling through international marketplaces is the easiest way to export your products. You might not expect there will be a demand for your items in far-flung countries like Australia, but many sellers with ordinary products like me have found a lot of success selling internationally.

Double-edged loyalty

Shoppers keep coming back to marketplaces, especially on Amazon if they are Prime members. This thus creates a constant flow of potential new customers for sellers. The only issue is that marketplaces does not necessarily foster customer retention for individual retailers, as re-marketing opportunities are slim or non-existent, nevertheless as a smart seller, play your way round it to get committed buyers.

Marketplaces also provide sellers with piles of data of their sales to learn how they are faring in the marketplaces.

Integration with third party tools

Just because you are selling on a marketplace does not mean that your favorite optimization tools will no longer work. From inventory management to pricing software, the best tools carry over to the marketplace of your choosing so that your selling experience can be the best possible.

GRADUATE TO YOUR OWN E-COMMERCE SITE

Now that you have succeeded in setting your market in some major marketplaces, I think it is now best if you set up your own e-commerce store. You have made so many contacts, friends and gained a number of buyers. If you are actually a smart seller, you will by now have email contacts of your buyers (this is possible with eBay) as they give sellers access to buyers' details including their email addresses. On the part of Amazon, email addresses of buyers are blocked, while they allow access to buyers' addresses. What I did was to create a spreadsheet where I saved the addresses.

Now that I'm at the advanced stage of completing my online e-commerce store, I have already prepared flyers that I will be sending out to those buyers introducing them to my own website while at the same time thanking them for their purchases on my store at Amazon. This is to enable the buyers know that I did not come across their addresses by accident. Here are the advantages of having your own website.

Hosting your own e-commerce site gives you more control over the shop and its presentation (better for business branding, makes moving to another web host easier, and can be more cost effective). You will possibly avoid transaction and listing fees leaving you only with processing fees like PayPal fees, Amazon payment, which is minimal anyway. You will be able to charge buyers more and you are not in direct competition with other sellers.

When buyers come to your website, they can only buy your item, which is a huge advantage to sellers who are used to very tough competition on Amazon and other marketplaces.

Eliminating your competitors

You will not lose sales to competitors who are selling the same item as you for a lesser price.

You can actually increase your prices because unlike Amazon, you do not have to drive your prices down and compete with sellers who seem to be able to sell items for a lot less than you and this results in bigger profits every time you make a sale on your website.

Branding

I will like to end this write up with branding which is the benefit you will have when you own your e-commerce website. While Amazon and other marketplaces will immediately bring you millions of potential customers, no buyer will remember your name or brand as what a customer will remember is that they bought it on Amazon/ eBay.

Having your own e-commerce website, however, immediately helps you build up your brand. Buyers will remember your web address and possibly refer people back to your company if they like your product or your services. Your company will grow in popularity rather than remain stagnant.

The next phase will be about Affiliate Marketing.

AFFILIATE MARKETING

What is Affiliate Marketing?

Affiliate marketing is the process of earning a commission by promoting other people's (or company's) products. You find a product you like, promote it to others, and earn a piece of the profit for each sale that you make. There are many affiliate companies like Commission Junction, Clickbank, JVzoo and more. All these affiliate companies provide opportunities for you to advertise other companies' products/services, whereas in the case of Amazon, it handles this by itself. It is called "Associate Programme" on Amazon UK, while the term "Affiliate" is used by Amazon US.

In most cases, you find products related to your niche or that you like, write about it on your website or blog. You will then promote the products and post a link on your site where potential buyers can click and purchase the products if they like it. When someone follows the link to buy something, you earn a commission. The commissions can either be a percentage of the sale or a fixed amount. For example, if I have a membership site or even an e-commerce store and invited people to become my affiliates. If you become one of my affiliates and make a commission, you get paid based on the agreement that I have made with you.

Your earnings are usually tracked by using a link that has a code embedded in it. This link is only used by you. Listed below are a few factors that help make your affiliate marketing successful:

☐ The amount of traffic you have, the higher the traffic, the greater your earning potential will be.
☐ The quality of the products you recommend. Recommending junk products will not make you sales so you want to make sure you recommend products that are of good quality and that people want to buy.
☐ The amount of trust readers has in you, so you must have an established trust to really make people to click the link on your blog.

Benefits of Affiliate Marketing

If you are looking for a way to make money online, you should consider affiliate marketing as there are numerous benefits to becoming an affiliate marketer. These include:

- There's no production cost; if you wanted to set up a business selling products online as I have discussed above, you will have to buy, ship and store the products. However, with an affiliate program, there is nothing like production cost, stock, etc. as the merchant does all these.

- The set up cost is low – you probably already have a desk, an internet connection and a computer. You will only have to buy traffic in order to drive targeted buyers to the products you are promoting.

- There are no fees or licenses to pay as affiliate programs are usually free to join. Your geographic market reach is as big as your ability to promote your site. The internet is a worldwide marketplace; you can take advantage of this market.

- You can promote almost anything, almost everything you can think of is sold online. There are thousands of affiliate programs, so it is easy to find products related to your site or blog.

- There is no need to handle any sales to make money, no inventory, no order processing and no shipping to deal with. You make money from sales by promoting the products, not having to take care of the actual sales process.

- Enables you to work from home, if you have ever had a long commute to work, you can really appreciate the ability to work from home. Affiliate marketing is also a great way to spend more time with your family. You won't also need the normal work expenses like transportation, buying lunch, increasing your wardrobe, etc. as you work from home in the comfort of your pajamas if you want.

- If you have your computer with you, you can work from anywhere in the world. Have you ever wanted to go on holiday, but getting approval to go is difficult? This is easy with this type of business as you do not need anyone's permission to travel moreover you can take your business with you on the trip as the only thing you need is either your tablet, laptop with an internet connection. Take your office with you and you won't have to spend more than a few hours a day working, and you could still visit anywhere you wanted while working.

- There is a minimal level of risk as if you try to sell a product and it is not making money, you just stop promoting that product and look for other profitable products to market, it is that simple. You don't have to worry about being stuck in a long-term contract that binds you to promote a product that doesn't sell.

There is potential for high income if you are willing to put in a little bit of effort with some paid advertising and regularly connecting with people on the social media platforms.

Benefits of becoming an Amazon Affiliate

Amazon is the world's biggest retailer online, and the best thing about them is that they are sharing their profits! You can make money while they are making money too.

The Amazon Associate Program provides compensation to their affiliate members who are referring customers to purchase on Amazon. They are offering a profitable opportunity for everyone to earn a huge amount of money.

Amazon is a world trusted brand. To prove, Nielson Research reported that Amazon is the most trusted brand worldwide and number one most popular shopping destination online. Amazon has millions of loyal customers all over the world and they spend more money in this online shopping marketplace than any other retailing site.

By being an affiliate member of Amazon, you will get a commission to the products you refer people to. The good thing is that a huge number of Amazon's online customers normally purchase more than one product per session. For this reason, as an affiliate member, you will not only earn a commission on the product that you are promoting for people to buy, but your commission will be based on all the products that they bought once they are on Amazon.

The commission on Amazon begins at 4% and can increase up to 15%. If you just sell 4 products per month, your commission will increase to 6%. The compensation goes like this, the more products you sell per month, then the higher your commission will be. Imagine if you have a lot of customers and they are purchasing more than one product at Amazon, the commission you can obtain when the payday comes will certainly be a big amount of money.

Amazon associates is straightforward and dependable. Once you sign up and provide the details of how you will like to be paid (check, direct deposit or gift certificate) you will receive your payments once you reach or cross the pre-established threshold limit (e.g. £100 with a two-month delay for the payment). If you move enough sales, after two months, you will be receiving a steady monthly payment from Amazon.

Amazon has an unlimited amount of inventory/products that are extremely reputable and which buyers are willing and ready to purchase. So, you don't have to promote belly fat secrets on your site or blog to make a buck. There are hundreds and thousands selection of high quality items that you can select and promote. You can promote only items that you truly believe are worth your readers' time and investment or better still, you can promote products based on your experience at reading a book or consuming a product.

Amazon is a master at converting visitors to customers as it spends millions of dollars in research to optimize the amount of sales they squeeze out of new and existing customers. I'm sure you will know if you have ever bought anything from Amazon, you are a customer for life as you will be receiving emails upon emails about products that they think you need, like, you might have bought an item this way as a result of the email ads based on the recommendation from Amazon. So all you really need to do is send people to the site and they will do the good job themselves for the most part.

The percentage of your commission raises in a given month as you sell more items as the more products you sell, the greater the percentage of your total sales will be. You will start at a very low 4% but you can actually reach the 8% range in a short period of time.

Number of Products Shipped/Downloaded in a Given Month**	Volume-Based Advertising Fee Rates for General Products
1-6	4.00%
7-30	6.00%
31-110	6.50%
111-320	7.00%
321-630	7.50%
631-1570	8.00%
1571-3130	8.25%
3131+	8.50%

The more products you are able to sell, the better your commission.

Below are the commission details at the time of this publication:

Standard Advertising Fee Structure

Amazon UK Site Standard Advertising Fee Rates

Product Category	Fixed Advertising Fee Rates
TV, Smartphones	1.0%
Video Games	2.5%
PC, Consumer Electronics	3.0%
Kindle (all devices), Musical Instruments, Major Appliances, Kitchen, Toys, Home improvement, DVD, Software, Digital products	5.0%
Office products, Home, Sports, Music, MP3, Baby, Personal Care Appliances & HPC, Grocery, Gift cards, Books	6.0%
Pet Products, Automotive, Lawn and Garden, Beauty, Amazon Local	7%
Shoes, Jewellery, Apparel, Watches, Luggage	10.0%
All other Products	5.0%

Sign Up and Play by The Rules

The first most important thing that you should do is to sign up to become an Amazon Affiliate:

Once Amazon approves your application, you will be given an access to a special section on their site, which will give you many different ways on how you can link to the official website of Amazon or the products they sell. After that, you will have to create affiliate links in your website, which will lead directly to Amazon or any product that they are selling on their site.

If the visitor of your site clicks in any of your approved affiliate links which automatically takes them to Amazon website, and they bought any item at Amazon within the given time period which is stated in the affiliate agreement, you earn a percentage of commission for that successful purchase.

As with the affiliate program, you need to follow strictly the terms of agreement, and be sure to promote the affiliate links in your site according to the affiliate agreement.

Take Note: If you will not follow correctly the terms of agreement of the affiliate program of Amazon, you will be removed from it and you will lose all the commission that you have earned since the time you have started as an affiliate associate. (For example, buying from Amazon using your own approved affiliate links may be a good idea as you will be able to get a discount, but for your information this is considered as a violation of Amazon's terms of agreement.)

There are others more so read and understand the terms of agreement. In this way, you will be able to make sure that you can continue earning money from the affiliate program of Amazon.

Choose a niche where profit is present

If you want to make sure that you will make money with Amazon Affiliate Program, one of the most important things that you should do is to choose the right niche. This is not all about selecting a niche with which you are interested to engage, but this is particularly about choosing a niche where there is profit and where you have a good information.

There are some theories online on how to choose a good niche on Amazon, but the best way to find a profitable niche is to select one that is reasonably new, has a good market demand or search volume and priced at a reasonable amount.

Another effective way for you to find a profitable niche is to identify your passion. Take, for example, you are passionate about books, you can go to Amazon and find out the most in demand books nowadays and promote them. If you want, you can easily find a good niche by checking out the bestsellers on Amazon. Go to their website, in the search box, click the arrow pointing down just beside it and a list of products by category will appear. Select the category that you want to engage with and click "Go."

Below the search box, there are a number of options to choose from for a better search result. There you will see the "Best Sellers" option, click it and it will show you the most in demand products in that particular category.

When you find a potential niche where there is profit, start building a good blog regarding this niche. You can start by building a free blog with Wordpress and Blogger. There are 2 wordpress platforms, one is free to use (wordpress.com), the other is not as you require the service of a hosting company (wordpress.org). You will need to decide which option is best for you. With free version, there is restricted service.

If you want the paid version (wordpress.org), you can get started by getting your own server from HostGator or BlueHost, or other hosting providers on the market.

Once you already have a blog, start researching for a good keyword that is relevant to your niche using keyword research tool such as Google AdWords or Market Samurai for better search results. Consider those niche relevant keywords that have high searches and low competition. And if you find a good keyword for your niche, start making an article about it and use it to promote a certain product by putting a simple, yet enticing hyperlink message directing to Amazon or the particular product you are promoting. In this way, you will be able to increase your chance to drive your visitors to purchase the product you are promoting on Amazon.

With a good write-up about a product describing the features, benefits, etc., this is an inducement to your reader to click the link on your article to go to Amazon to find out more about this product which you have written a review about and probably make a purchase which will earn you a commission.

Create a product review site or blog review site

One of the most effective ways that affiliate marketers use to make money at Amazon is by creating a blog review or product review website for the items that they would like to promote and earn commission.

A blog review, for example, is a great way to convince or drive the visitors of your site to visit Amazon and make a purchase. Once you found a list of products to promote on Amazon or any other reliable sources, write an enticing and honest review about them. The write-up/review may have been a result of your own experience with the use of the item or of others.

Tell something that will educate your readers about the product such as the advantages of it, the benefits it can provide and so on as well as how that product can serve as a big help for them when they use it. In addition, include also some attractive facts such as discounts or money back guarantee. This will help you to encourage your readers to try the product and buy it at Amazon.

Take Note: Your new site cannot work on its own to attract online customers to visit your blog. You need to promote your site in order for you to be visited by potential customers.

Promote your blog by article marketing, forum marketing, social bookmarking, social media marketing, and other effective online marketing strategies which must include paid advertising using either google AdWords, Facebook, solo ads or all.

Choose the right product to promote

The most ideal products to promote are those items that are in demand at this time. The rule here is simple: if the product is in demand, promote it, but if not, then don't. Don't risk your time for products that are not getting any good sales, if there are those sale-able products available for you to choose from. Be wise!

One of the best ways for you to choose a good product to promote is to be updated with the hottest trends. Anything that is currently advertised on the television or radio is an ideal product to promote online.

You can watch popular shows to know the products that the show is promoting. Popular and reputable shows that are really influential, so when they promote the product of their guest, viewers tend to purchase it. Use Google Trends, Click bank and others to research hottest products in demand.

Considered as the easiest method, another effective way for you to find an ideal product to promote is to go to the official website of Amazon then check out their bestselling products. Find a good product to promote that is related to the niche that you want.

Aside from these, you can also find an ideal product to promote by reading blog reviews or product review sites. Choose those products that has a lot of good customer reviews online.

Other means of promoting your offers

- Videos – if you don't like writing, perhaps making a video might work better for you. You can tell your viewers about the benefits of the product, post the video to YouTube, monetize it by using paid adverts to get quality and numerous views.

- Articles, you can get someone else to write an article about the product for you. The popular and cheapest place to get articles is fiverr.com. Post the article on your blog with your affiliate link, submit it to article directories, they are tons of them such as e-zine articles and more. Just go to Google to search for article directories.

- Social media, the benefits of social media are endless. If you don't have a social media page of some kind such as Facebook, twitter or LinkedIn, you need to have these three at most. You can write a short post or make a note which you will post into the social media and tweet about the product on your twitter account. If you are not on the social media, you are missing a lot.

- Solo Ads – you can find a list that is a good fit for your product/service with an audience that will be interested in it and use solo ads for that product.

Google AdWords – buy advertising with google AdWords to drive traffic to your videos, reviews, etc. If you can afford it, you may wish to use Yahoo and Bing too in order to earn decent commissions every month.

Put the Amazon links on the right place

Typically, for you to make money on this affiliate program of Amazon, your visitors should go to your website, click the valid affiliate links to be directed to Amazon, and buy from them. However, placing the approved link in the wrong location will lessen your chance to make money.

The key here for you to succeed and earn money from this affiliate program is to put your approved affiliate links in the right place. It is very important to strategically put your Amazon Affiliate Links on your website in order for you to obtain the best results.

Take Note: Your chance to make money with Amazon Affiliate Program will depend on the location of your affiliate links on your website. Putting the affiliate links on the right place, the higher your chance to drive a visitor of your site to purchase from Amazon.

Some of the most effective ways for you to maximize your potential to make money from Amazon Affiliate Program is to put your approved links on banners, sidebar widgets and articles or product reviews on your site. These are the best of all possible placements on your website, and these are the top locations that high earning affiliate members are putting their approved links.

To be particular, here are the most effective Amazon linking methods you can use to your full advantage.

Product Links – This method enables you to display a number of product images with descriptions arising from the keywords that you have selected. This linking method will ensure that the products showed in your site are relevant to your niche.   The nice thing with this is that you have the ability to control and modify the size of the display box according to your preference as well as its colour.

Example product link (text and image):

Text and image

Image only

large

Kindle Fire HD 7

medium

small

Search Box – Placing a search box on your site that your visitors can use to search for products at Amazon is also a good linking method. If they found a product and followed the link to Amazon to purchase it, then you get commission for this.

Content Links – This Amazon linking method enables you to put a text link within a certain part of your article, which will lead to Amazon or to the page where the particular product that you are promoting is located. For example, perhaps you wrote an article or review about Samsung Galaxy. You can hyperlink word Samsung Galaxy using the exact URL of that product on Amazon, so that when the readers click on it, they will be directed to it on Amazon.

Slide Show – This is one of the most effective linking methods available as it can easily attract the visitors of your site to check the product and go to Amazon.

In this method, you just have to simply choose the products that you want to promote and they will eventually be displayed in the slide show in a rotating order.

The moving products from the slide show can certainly get the attention of the visitors of your site, which in turn increases the chance that they will click them and take time to check them out on Amazon. Maximize your full potential to make money online with the use of this Affiliate Program. Use this guide to help you succeed in making money with Amazon Affiliate Program.

If you want to ensure that you will make money with Amazon Affiliate Program, follow these things mentioned above and incorporate them properly. In this way, you will be able to make sure that you will earn higher amounts of money from being an affiliate of Amazon. In addition, you might have to take some affiliate training programs where you can learn how to be successful with affiliate marketing. If you really want to learn more as it is not possible to write about all in this book, connect with me and I will show you.

The last but not the least is Kindle Publishing which covers the rest of the chapters in this book.

KINDLE PUBLISHING

Many businesses and services have jumped on the eBook band wagon and achieved success by publishing them online. EBooks can be written about any subject or topic you feel your viewers would love to read.

You can even hire others to write your eBooks for you if you'd like. I have found, however, that writing your own eBooks and publishing them on Amazon Kindle is another wonderful and profitable way for you to build any business or service you operate and make money with Amazon.

Don't freak out if you're not technologically savvy. You don't have to be. In this book, you will learn how to write a good eBook, add a little "Kindling" and get your business off to a burning success!

What is a Kindle?

Unless you have been living in an extremely remote part of the world, you have probably heard of a Kindle Fire, but you might not know exactly what it is and how it operates.

The Kindle is a mini tablet. Technically, it's computer version of the Kindle eBook reader that runs a forked version of Google's Android system.

The cost of a Kindle 'Fire' averages around £129, which means with a price that low, more and more people are going to want to own them. Other great features of the Kindle Fire include:

8 GB of internal storage Software • Android 4.0 operating system • Access to the Amazon Appstore • Cloud-accelerated split browser • Large variety of formats supported such as: Kindle Format 8 Kindle Mobi, PDF, TXT, PRC natively, unrestricted MOBI, PRC natively, Audible/Audible Enhanced AA, AAX, JPEG, PNG, nonDRM AAC, DOC, DOCX, GIF, BMP, MP3, OGG, MIDI, MP4, WAV, and VP8.

Benefits of a Kindle

As you can see, the Kindle Fire is an awesome piece of technology. That alone makes people want to have one. It also has many other benefits that make it perfect for your choice to publish your eBook. Never thought of publishing an ebook on Kindle before? Don't worry. If you follow the ideas in this book, you will be a published author before you know it.

Here are just a few of the totally awesome features to show what a benefit owning a Kindle Fire can do for your book as these are reasons why people buy the Fire and use it instead of paper copy books:

- Cost effective - As stated above, it is inexpensive. More and more people want to own one because it is much cheaper than the Apple iPad. This gives you a larger customer base. People will be looking for eBooks, and this is one of the greatest platforms of them in the world.

- Simplicity of use - To say "it's so easy a child could do it," would seem like a cliché. Even though it seems that way, it is that easy to use. In fact, it is so easy that many parents purchase them for their children, so it's perfect for every level of eBook you could choose to write. You can write serious adult eBooks or the youngest child eBook and publish it on Kindle.

- Number of Apps - You get many more apps for much less money from Amazon. The selection is huge and they're yours to choose from.

- Movies - You can actually play movies from places like Netflix. This may not seem like much for a writer, but it is just another feature that makes someone want to have a Kindle

Fire. The more people who own one, the greater the chance they will see your eBook.

- Free PDF delivery - You can download files over Wi-Fi at absolutely no cost to you. Many companies charge fees for things like this, but Amazon does not.

- Fast Dual-Core Processor - The processor is a state-of-the art, dual-core processor. It makes it much more powerful. With this you can actually stream music while you are reading books or browse the web while you download videos. It is like multitasking abilities on steroids.

- Battery life - Battery life has always been a problem when it comes to technology. I absolutely hate the life of my cell phone battery. I play a lot, do a bit of work, or at my leisure, play a few games and before I know it, I get that the battery signal is low. With the Kindle, you get a 50% better battery life - that's right - 50%. Who could ask for more than a battery with a contrast ratio that good?

- Wi-Fi audible delivery - You no longer need a computer to transfer audible audio books. It can be done over Wi-Fi for a much faster speed. No more lugging that computer around from place to place just so you could download things you felt were important. With the Wi-Fi audible delivery, Amazon has made it easy.

- Improved PDF enhancement - Their PDF reader can now support six contrast options. It also has a cursor so you can highlight words. Contrast options are great for giving anything you create a bright, crisp color.

- Monitoring Download - This allows a user to watch their eBooks download in real time. You don't have to wait and wait and wait for a download forever. I know it takes quite a bit of time and it is often time wasted. Being able to watch them download in real time, however, solves that problem.

- Full-Screen Texts - Those reading eBooks can now use the auto-hide feature which gives you more room for texts. This is especially nice for those who are getting older and need larger text to see clearly.

- Two dictionaries are included - You can look up words you want to use in two different styles of dictionaries to inform you of just the answer you were seeking.

- Free Cloud Storage - On many devices, as your memory fills, your machine slows down. I know people who are bad to save things on their computer until it comes to a rapid halt. Then they have to take things off and move them to different files. Or put them on flash drives. With the Kindle Fire, those days are gone, because they give you Amazon Cloud to store all your digital content. Ah aah, the power of the Cloud!

The Amazon Kindle Fire is the most popular tablet of its kind right now for many reasons. Since it is the most popular device for people around the world, it makes excellent sense to publish your eBook there. Sometimes, you put your heart and soul into the eBook you want to write. When you do that, you want to give your eBook every opportunity for success that you can, and publishing on Kindle is the best opportunity around. Your book will stay safe in the Cloud as your profits rise to meet it.

Quick looks at hot topics

Perhaps now things are beginning to heat up in your mind and you are beginning to see how valuable publishing on Kindle can be. Maybe you're playing around with the thought to actually write an eBook in your mind, but you just haven't got a clue what to write about. Amazon makes researching hot topics extremely easy for you to do with just a few simple steps.

- First of all, you just simply have to visit http://www.amazon.com/Kindle-eBooks to get started.

- Select a category - Whatever your niche is, simply look for that type of book. You don't have to have a huge business to develop an eBook. As a matter of fact, you don't have to have a business started at all. Maybe you just enjoy baking and would like to publish a cookbook for fast and easy desserts to publish and sell. Simply select the category "cookbooks." You will see many, but don't get discouraged.

- Select a subcategory - A list of subcategories will appear on the left side. Look for something such as "desserts or fast and easy" that applies to whatever it is you are writing about. If you see a lot in that category, you may want try some alternate sub categories, like low fat and delicious.

- View top sellers - This will give you a look at who the top sellers are in the category you want to write in. These are now the people who are considered to be the experts in that particular field. It does not mean you can't be the next one.

- Select an eBook - Actually click on one of the eBooks from that list. It can be just any eBook that catches your eye.

- Rank - Look down the page after you click on the book and find the "Amazon Best Sellers Rank." This lets you know who the best sellers at this time are.

- Use the ranks to guide you - Ranks can be a helpful tool for you. They will let you know what was paid in the Kindle Store at the current time of writing. If there have been a lot of eBooks sold, then generally, these are the types of eBooks people enjoy reading and are willing to spend their money on. Once you have established that people like to buy eBooks based on the niche you have chosen, no matter what that niche is, then you can be confident that if you produce one with quality content, that it will sell. Don't think, "Oh, there's too many and no one will want mine."

- Think instead - "How can I create an ebook that is so awesome they will overlook others and come looking for mine."

If you think only expert eBook writer should publish on Amazon Kindle, you're mistaken. You may be the CEO of your own company that is already doing quite well. Writing and publishing on Kindle can help you grow your business even more.

Don't see how you could write an eBook and use it to improve the success of your company? It really is quite simple. If you are the owner or CEO of a big business, you probably have many areas of expertise that you would love to be able to share with a reading audience.

Write down those assets you have and write down the things that your customers ask about the most. Match A to B, and you have got it – that is the content for your eBook. By simply selecting one aspect of your expertise and matching it to the information your customers want, you can determine if the books will sell well on that topic. If those types are selling, you can begin writing your eBook, and get it out there by promoting it.

Every sale or hit to your book should link to your site. It will increase traffic for your website, and even more greatly improve your chance of business success. It's an awesome way to get your business out there to more people not only in your area or even your country, but around the entire world. After all, we truly live in a world-wide marketplace.

Getting Started

Amazon Kindle Publishing is a great place to be a part of when you are ready to begin. Below is a step by step guide on how to join and how to get an account through Amazon KDP Publishing. Go to http://kdp.amazon.com. When you type the web address, this is what you will get

Below the login box, you will see preferences for languages from where you can select the language of your choice. After this, click the sign up button and on the next screen, enter your email address, tick the "I am a new customer" radio button.

On the registration page, make sure that you enter the following information:

- Your name
- Your email address
- Re-typed email address
- The password you prefer
- Re-typed password

Then, click the create account button. After this, you will see the Kindle Direct Publishing Terms of Service (TOS). Please make sure you read the TOS so that you will avoid any unnecessary problems in the future. Once you have read and understood the terms, click the "agree" button. You will then be taken to another similar page only that this window is meant for Amazon EU websites. Make sure you read it anyway for further information and click the "agree" button.

You will then be redirected to the Kindle Direct Publishing main page. On the same page, pay close attention to the yellow box on the top right hand corner and it will read something like:

"Your account information is incomplete. To publish a book, you will need to complete this. Update now"

When you click on the update now hyperlink will redirect you to the account information page. The page will contain the following sections:

Company/Publisher Information

This is the section that identifies you as an individual who wants to publish an eBook. If you have a company that is engaged in the publishing business, you can use it as the business name otherwise enter your name.

Tax Information

Here is the section for tax reporting purposes. Remember, more especially if you live in the US that royalties earned from the sale of your eBook needs to be reported to the IRS for tax purposes.

Royalty Payment

This section deals with the markets catered to by Amazon. The first marketplace is the global site while the latter ones are under Amazon EU. If you aim at getting your eBook seen under the Amazon EU marketplaces, you can then click the + (plus) sign after each marketplace to expand it. Remember to click the "add a bank account" link to enter your bank account information. Amazon usually start remitting your royalties electronically 60 days after your book start selling. However, if you do not want to enter your bank account information, you will receive your royalty payment by cheque.

When you are done, check all of your entries to make sure they are correct and click the "save button"

Put your eBook together

I hope you're getting excited about the possibility of writing your own eBook and publishing it on Kindle now. You at least know WHY you SHOULD do it. If you're worried about how to do it, it's easier than you may think. Remember, everyone hates first things. I remember the first time one of my lecturers in the University invited me to his office. My knees shook the whole way there as I have no clue of what to expect. I kept going over that very small list of things he may have considered wrong. I was so shook up I did not think I'd make it through the door, I did, and to my utter shock, he was just there to advise me that I was very good at writing and should consider "writing" as a hobby. As at that time, I just laughed it off, but today, things are changing as I'm really into the writing business.

Was I relieved? The point is, I got myself all worked up over nothing. If you're getting worked up about writing an eBook, you're getting worked up over nothing. It really is not that difficult do you understand?

Many people never take the opportunity to explore the possibility of eBooks because they just don't feel they have what it takes to write a book. When you write eBooks, however, it's a bit different. You're not looking for a 300-page novel. Some eBooks are only about 20 pages long. A good one will probably be at least 30-40 pages. There is, however, no limit. They can be as long or as short as you want them to be or as long or as short as you feel they need to be (most are just 1, 200 words) and will still convey what you want the readers to learn.

The length often depends on whether or not you're publishing them to sell or publishing them to give away as part of an email marketing campaign, with another purchase, or to special customers, however, it can be both. That choice is determined by you.

Perhaps you just want to begin writing and write until you have said all you want or need to say to get the message across that you want to portray to your audience. Sometimes, when you begin your first eBook, writing until you have said it all may be the best thing to do. After you have said it all, go back and edit and add more clarity for the reader. Before you know it, you have knocked out more pages than you thought possible. If it is a topic you are passionate about, that won't take long at all to do.

Writing your eBook

Writing in general has a process. It does not matter if you are writing an essay for school, a report of some kind, a story, etc. Each one takes a certain process which needs to be done thoroughly. It does not matter if it is an article, essay, eBook, or a novel, the general steps are the same. Though eBooks do have a different medium of publication from other books, in most ways, they look alike. For this reason, they are written using the same steps. Here is what you need to do to begin your journey of becoming an eBook author.

Decide your target market

Before you write, you have to know who is going to be reading it. You may be selling it to peers in your industry looking to advance in the field. Maybe you're writing an exercise book for women/men. It could be a cookbook for anyone who loves to cook or a "Macho Man" grilling cookbook. Whoever you feel will benefit from your book is your target market, those are the ones you write "to." You must use a writing style which they can relate to and that will attract them.

Create a roadmap

There are many ways to approach an idea and many directions to head in once you get started. Which roads you take will be totally up to you. If you want to write an instructional book, you may decide to write the book and accompany it with a workbook to increase its marketability. The workbook can be extremely important and can also increase your sales.

You're giving someone a deal by accompanying your book on the topic with a workbook, so you're giving them value for their money. As you plan the book, plan which sections of the book will go with what worksheet and decide the order and layout of each book. You'd be surprised how easy it is to come up with worksheets. It can even be fun being that creative.

Often, writing an outline of the book will help you stay organized. I will caution you, if you're a "technical" kind of person, which will be further discussed later, try to plan your idea around language that all people can understand.

Build on a main idea

Once your idea and plan are together, it is time to build on that idea and get further toward the goal of writing. You have got all the tools you need for success. You know the key concepts you want to get across and what order you want them in.

Take each concept you want to portray in each section of your book and just write a good sentence about it. Then, build on each of these content sentences until you have fully discussed that concept. Then, you can simply move on to others.

If you want to write a fiction eBook, you will have to consider different ideas when creating your plan such as the plot, characters, scene, etc. That will be part of your plan. You'll have to develop each character and design every scene in your head as you prepare to write.

When you write an eBook, it's a lot different than writing the average novel, because it's open to self-publishers at little or no cost to them. The average eBook will probably be too short to print, but definitely long enough that you can develop a valid eBook. That is why it's perfectly fine to even write your eBook using a simple idea. Writing fiction for a child is even available, so just take your best shot.

Organize your details

The approach you use in building on your plan will vary depending on the subject matter. If you're writing a self-help book or maybe your memoirs, the use of an outline works very well. Another way to build is to write down everything you can think of and then draw a web with lines going from each topic.

You have completed brainstorming and writing an outline or a web of ideas, you probably have quite a bit of information about your topic on paper. Look at the information and decide exactly how you feel your book should flow. The order of your book can be important to a reader. It needs to have an even flow and not bounce back from place to place.

Think of what your reader needs to know in the beginning. What do they need to know that is imperative for them to understand before they begin? Put that information at the start of your book. Once your readers get the beginning concepts, they will be ready to work on more difficult concepts or medium-level concepts.

Save the very difficult concepts for the end. A mechanic would never teach someone to rebuild an engine before he learned to rotate a tire. If you try too hard to push difficult things too early, you may lose them.

If you're writing a self-help eBook on cooking, for example, you can divide each chapter easily by the type of food you're cooking. Some are done by meal such as "Breakfast, Lunch, Dinner, and Dessert." Others do it by the type of food such as "Italian, French, Mexican, etc." Ordering other eBooks may be a little more difficult to do, but having your order thought out is extremely important.

Just write!

Now comes the fun part -writing! You don't need any special equipment to write your book. You can use Microsoft Office Word, or OpenOffice to write it. Don't stress out about what you want to title it or any other elements of the book, just write it (The title can actually be the last thing which you will have to brainstorm or even ask friends/family of the best title for your eBook).

Every book of any kind has three main sections: Introduction, body, and conclusion. The introduction introduces your topic. The body is the information, story, directions, etc. of your book. The conclusion touches on key points mentioned and leaves the writer feeling the book is complete.

Since the introduction is where they'll start reading, you want to start with something that really catches their attention. Then you "wow" them with your content. In the end, you want to leave the reader with an emotion. It does not matter what the emotion is: Happy, proud, sad, a sense of contentedness or achievement, and in some fiction books, even anger. Why? You have made them feel something.

When you can write well enough to provoke an emotion from them, you know you have touched them, and that is going to make them glad they read your book. They will want more, and they will be happy to let their friends know about your eBook.

There are different ways to write. Many start at the beginning and go straight through to the end. Others like to start in the middle where they're more comfortable with the content and write the beginning and ending when they're satisfied they have gotten their meaning right.

They use their introduction to write into the middle and their conclusion to summarize key points leading out of the middle. Whichever method you choose; you must be committed to it. If it is not working for you, then just try another until you find which technique works for you. Don't be surprised if you find yourself doing different books differently. Depending on the topic, sometimes it's easier to even start at the bottom and build up.

You are not going to sit down and write your first eBook overnight. It takes time to write a book, even if it is a shorter one like an eBook, it is extremely important that you don't give up on yourself! This book actually took me longer than I thought and this can be the situation with you but do not give up, you will surely complete it. Once you compete the 1st eBook successfully, others will follow with more confidence.

If you feel your confidence swaying, and your determination to press on is slipping away, let it go for a bit. Don't try to push yourself into an all-day thing. You may want to set a little bit of time aside each day that is just for writing. You may want to write until you reach a particular word count (This is what I do).

When you reach your goal, then get up from your desk and either stop for the day, or take a break. You'd be surprised how just writing something down, even if you don't feel it's so great, can get your creative juices flowing again.

Editing

When you finish the book, don't look at it for a few days. After a few days, pick it up and look over it again more critically.   Check the book carefully to be sure you still think all the sections and chapters are ordered and placed in the right order. It is often common to think that some parts of the book would maybe make a little better sense somewhere else. You can cut, paste, and revise until you have it in the perfect order.

Editing takes a good deal of time. Sure, it's not as much time as actually writing, but it's still a good idea to pace yourself. You can edit by a number of pages, number of chapters, or even the number of words whatever works for you.

Just like sections or chapters needed moved around, you will find words that you need to rearrange or reword. You may have to move sentences around to keep related ideas together.

There's an old saying that "deletion is the soul of editing." If something just does not seem to feel right and you can't seem to revise it so it fits, it is often best to just delete it. If you're reading it and you say, "Huh?" Then your reader probably will too. If it is information you feel you have to keep in, just put it away for a while and try to fit it in again in another manner at a later time.

Once you finish your book, you will need to look for a good proof reader who will edit the script professionally to make it look appealing to your reading audience.   You can get a good proof reader from guru.com, upwork.com, freelancer.com or if you have a low budget, head straight to fiverr.com. That Fiverr is cheap does not mean you won't get a good and quality proof reader you just have to do a little digging to uncover the best proof reader freelancer.

Detail refinement

When you are confident that the body of your book is exactly what you want, it is time to fine tune and detail your book. There will be things you want to add at this time such as any introduction or conclusion points you feel need added. This is what I do and that is why I'm advising you to do so too, though it is not mandatory as you may prefer to do it differently. You will also want a bibliography and maybe a table of contents. The TOC is not always necessary, but if it is a detailed, self-help or how to book, it often helps the reader find exactly the sections they are looking for.

Now, you need a very important part of your book…the title. Sometimes, you know right away what you want to title a book. I have written books around great titles. Often times the title may come to you while you are writing the book. Other times, you sit around with an untitled book waiting for a name. Several titles may come to you over the course of time you spend writing the book. Remember when you consider your title, it has to do a few things:

1. Give the reader an idea as to the book's topic.
2. Catch the reader's attention.
3. Contains keywords for your potential customer's search.

If you get stuck, take a break. When you come back to it, you may want to play around with the title for a few days. Turn to family or friends you trust and run your ideas by them for their more objective viewpoints. When you're sure you have developed the perfect title, then you can add it to the eBook.

Make sure it is well proofread and edited. If you have an eBook that is filled with typographical and grammatical errors, you'll get negative customer reviews which will discourage other readers from purchasing your book.

Make sure your book description is compelling because this is where the reader gets the chance to learn about your book before they buy it. In your description, you have to be able to convince the reader that buying your book will be worth it. Also remember you can use limited HTML in your description such as bolding, italic and lists to make it look nicer to the eye.

Credits and citations

Often you use research from other people's works when you write your essay. You will need to add a bibliography sheet to your book, usually at the back, that gives properly cited information about the author of each source. Often times, your sources are just friends. If that is the case, you should also acknowledge them. There are several ways you can let you know how much you appreciated them, but it is important for you to write a special letter, name each one, and thank them for their help.

Cover

What often draws people to a book is not the title, but the cover itself. It is a good marketing tool to use when you write your eBook as well. Even though it is a virtual market, it still gives readers a chance to see the virtual cover and causes them to notice you over someone else with similar material.

Often, people will consider hiring someone to design their cover. Other times, they do it themselves. If you feel you can create something that will attract potential buyers, then give it a try. If you can't, maybe you have a friend who may have ideas. If not, there are professionals that will do it from freelance sites like fiverr.com upwork.com. Find one who has work you feel is comparable to what you want and hire them. It will be worth the effort. There are great places on line where you can get the use of "free" images.

An example of a free image site is www.sxc.hu. Just remember to do your due diligence and check their terms of use/guidelines for using their images.

A lot of people put a lot of effort into their covers and never seem to get them just right. This is where publishing on Kindle can really help you prepare that cover that WOWs the competitions. Kindle has a Cover Creator that can help you create and design your cover. They allow you to either use an image you provide, such as a picture, graphic or custom logo or to choose one of their stock images. You can customize your cover by using their selection of layouts and font sets. The process for doing this is easy. You just follow a few simple steps and you're up and running with your new published eBook:

1. Select "starting a new" cover -Just click on the existing book title or click on "Add new title" button. Next, you click "Design with Cover Creator." You'll find that in Section 4. "Upload Your Cover." Once you do that, the Cover Creator will take over, interface will launch, and you will be provided with directions as to what to do next.

2. Add the image of your own or from stock images -The image is the focal point of your cover design, so you should select it carefully. You want it to both tell what the book is about and be creative enough to draw a person's eye to it. If you provide your own image, you want to make sure it's an image that is of high quality. You must also have total rights to use the image on your cover.

3. Places like www.istockphoto.com and www.sxc.hu have a large number of awesome pictures and graphics you can use.

4. Select the design you want -There will be 10 design bases you can choose from once you have uploaded your picture. Go through each base and try your information on it to see what it looks like. Select the one you feel best shows off your information and graphics. After you select one, you can customize it with different layouts, fonts and color schemes. If you have come this far and still can't find an image you like, don't fret. If you can't find an image you feel portraits your eBook, you can find base designs that allow you to prepare a cover without an image.

5. Customize the layout - When you choose your base design, you can begin to customize the layout. It is easy to make changes of the fonts, colour schemes and layouts of texts. All you have to do when you feel something needs changed is to simply click separately on each part.

6. Preview your cover and submit it - Once you feel it is complete, all you have to do is click "Preview Cover." You can check to see how it looks in grayscale, color, and even thumbnail modes. Since Amazon uses those thumbnail pictures, it is more important that your picture looks best in the thumbnail

mode, not just full scale. If you find something you want to change, simply edit it. When you're pleased with the cover, all you have to do is click "Save & Submit." The Cover Creator will automatically close and load the cover. The cover will be loaded directly into the "Edit book details" of KDP.

You're not stuck with the cover. If at a later date you feel you want to change something, or come across a really cool image you feel is exactly what you were looking for you can simply click "Edit my Cover."
You will have to finalize again by continuing to the "Rights & Pricing page and then click on "Save and Publish."

If you prefer, you can also outsource the design of your eBook cover to places like www.Fiverr.com. The recommended size of the cover image you should get done is between 1,000 pixels and 2,500 pixels high and between 625 pixels and 1,563 pixels wide. Also, it's recommended that your cover image looks good and is readable if you convert it into a greyscale picture.

Format according to guidelines

When you begin preparing for publishing, there are a few things you should do beforehand. Gather all important information because the clearer the information you gather about your eBook, the easier it will be when you get it published. It will also make promoting it easier.

For publishing, you will want to have a separate piece of paper for notes as you retype certain things over and over. Write the title of eBook and the titles of any chapters or sections you have; how many sections or chapters you have; the word count of the total eBook, and; using that information develop a list of descriptive terms or keywords you feel relate to the book.

Publish your eBook on Kindle

You can potentially reach millions of readers across the world by simply publishing your book on Amazon's Kindle store. With eBook sales overtaking traditional book sales at book stores, it makes sense for author to harness the power of Amazon's Kindle store. Besides, what's not to love about ebooks? It is quick and easy to acquire and can be read like a book using a Kindle device or any other ebook reader or even on tablet, iPhone and android phones.

When you publish your eBook, you could become a vendor, but then you would have to deal with all the trips to the postal office to ship out each individual book sold. Instead, joining Kindle Direct Publishing or Amazon Advantage programs make your work a lot easier.

Now you're ready to start the publishing process to Amazon Kindle. Some of the above information can seem intimidating, and you may think it is difficult. Believe me, if I can figure out how to do it, then anyone can. Amazon has made it incredibly easy. They have a template you can use to get your book ready for publication at: http://self-publishing-coach.com/kindle-ebooktemplate.html. We're going to review their publishing guidelines, however, they have a site set up for you at: https://kdp.amazon.com/selfpublishing/help.

The first thing you need to do is simply go to http://kdp.amazon.com/. Here you can submit your ebook and fill in all the required details. They offer all the tools to create your content and upload it for free. When you publish with Kindle and give them your titles to sell for Amazon Kindle, they will send you payment for each eBook that is sold.

When you're ready to make the eBooks you have written available electronically to the world, you just use Kindle Direct Publishing (KDP). All you need to do is format your book in a one of their support formats. Here are a lot of key factors you should realize about publishing with Kindle:

1. If you choose the 70% royalty option, there will be no fees such as: sign-up, publishing, etc. You just earn 70% of the cost for each title that qualifies.

2. Publish one time and sell it everywhere. It will sell automatically on Kindle iPad, PC, Blackberry, iPhone, Mac, and Android phones.

3. You will be able to make a connection with the entire author community. They even have author forums if you go to their community pages at: http://forums.kindledirectpublishing.com.

4. If you have a short content eBook, you can submit the KDP published as a Kindle Single. Just email it to kindlesingles@amazon.com. You will need to include a description of the content of the eBook, the ASIN of the title, and their KDP email address.

5. If desired, you can self-publish the content of your eBook as either a blog or news feed through Kindle Publishing for Blogs.

Kindle publishing guidelines

Here are the guidelines required for publishing on Kindle:

- Read about the guidelines here - https://kindlegen.s3.amazonaws.com/AmazonKindlePublishingGuidelines.pdf

- Next, you download Kindle Plugin for Adobe InDesign —This helps you convert any eBooks or documents into a Kindle Format

- You will also need to install Adobe InDesign before you begin to install Kindle Plugin for Adobe InDesign - http://kindlegen.s3.amazonaws.com/KindlePluginForAdobeInDesign_PublishingGuidelines.pdf

- If you're a Mac user and you run OS X 10.6.7 or later, then you need to install VeriSign Class 3 Code Signing 2010 CA. This should be installed to the "System" Keychain before you install the plugin.

Kindle previewer download

The Kindle Previewer is a very effective tool and you should download it for sure. It helps imitate how books will display on all Kindle devices and applications. It also gives you a chance to be sure that the text displays correctly for all orientations or font sizes. It is highly recommended to help you produce a high-quality Kindle book.

You can get it for either Windows or Mac OSX platforms. Download it at http://www.amazon.com/kindleformat/kindlepreviewer.

Content guidelines

Following the guidelines set up by Kindle are very important. Everything from your title, cover art, description, and content, has to meet the guidelines. If not, Kindle has the right to decide if they feel the content is appropriate. They may opt to not offer it, or may even terminate your participation in the program if these guidelines are not met. Here are the guidelines:

- Pornography - Any pornography or offensive graphics showing sexual acts will not be accepted.

- Content that is Offensive - You can probably see by now what kind of content that would seem offensive.

- Illegal Content or Infringing Content - Laws and proprietary rights are taken very seriously by Kindle. You must understand that just because the content is available all over, does not mean you have the right to copy and sell it. You must be responsible enough to make sure your content is not in violation of any laws, trademark, copyright, publicity, privacy or any other types of rights.

- Non-Exclusive/Public Domain Content - There are many materials, like public domain content, that are free to use for everyone. Kindle does not accept content that is available freely unless you are the copyright owner. There really would not be any point in their trying to accept material to sell that is available free online. They accept public domain content, but the content has to be differentiated from the lots out there.

- Customer Experience is Poor - Kindle will not accept books that they feel would provide their customers with a poor experience such as: books with misleading titles, books that are poorly formatted, or if there is any cover art or product descriptions which are misleading. They have the right to decide whether or not your eBook will have poor customer experience.

- Formats – Amazon allow you to convert your draft for many different formats. If you want to get the best results, however, Amazon suggest that you upload in DOC/DOCX or HTML format. Formatting may seem difficult, but it really is not. Although they prefer the formats listed above, other formats are accepted. Listed below are other formats which is acceptable.

  - Word (DOC, DOCX) - Amazon accept this format, but if you have complex formatting, be aware that it may not convert well. You will want to use the previewer available so you can check the files conversion. If you are using tables or graphics, make sure the conversion shows up properly. If you are using Word, be aware that the font sizes, page numbers, and margin sets will not apply. If you want a page break somewhere, don't just enter a few times to make one. You need to intentionally use the "page break" feature on Word. That works best when you want to end a chapter because it will make for an easier transition and a better overall reading experience. You will need to upload the entire book text in one file.

  - HTML (ZIP, HTM, or HTML) - You must compress all files into one ZIP file before you upload it if your content contains any images. If you have images and you are using HTML for PC, you need to save it using Web Page, Filtered, (*HTM & *HTML) If you are using a MAC, then you save it using Web Page (.htm) (for Mac) This includes all the images. Then compress them into a ZIP file for upload. If you don't use images, you can simply upload the HTML file without compressing it.

- ePub (EPUB) You should validate your file by going to http://code.google.com/p/epubcheck to be sure it converts properly for Kindle. Kindle will convert ePub files that are unzipped.

- MOBI (MOBI) is the name given to the format developed for the MobiPocket Reader and currently used by Amazon with a slightly different DRM scheme. The free Calibre software tool that helps convert your HTML version ebook into MOBI format is available for free for Mac, PC & Linux at http://calibre-ebook.com

- Plain Text (TXT) - You can only use this when your book does not contain an image. KDP will convert all text to HTML for you, but if there are any images they will not display in the book

- Rich Text Format (RTF) - All of these files can be converted

- Adobe PDF (PDF) - Kindle does accept these files for eBook conversion. If the file contains any special formatting or even some images, they may not export well into the conversion process. Optical character recognition systems often find it difficult to interpret the special formatting that is embedded or the image placement. Many problems such as: irregular bolded texts or page breaks, inconsistent font sizes or text flow, and images that are either missing or oversized. If you have this problem, it is recommended that you convert your PDF to a DOC format.

How to determine the price for an eBook

Remember, as a Publisher Amazon allows you to set a price for your book publisher. When you are considering pricing an eBook, generally, the price will turn the most profit if you price them between $0.99 and $5.99 for each copy. It does not sound like a lot, but it gets written once, and can be sold for a small amount hundreds of times and for a life time. However, the power is not in the price of the book, it is actually in the volume of sales. When choosing your sales price, also keep Amazon's royalty structure in mind as a guide. If you will like to earn for example 70% royalties at Amazon.com, your minimum sales price needs to be $2.99. If you sell it between $0.99 and $2.98, you will earn 35% royalties.

It is important that you decide which way you want to go. Kindle offers you two royalty options when you publish yourself. They are 35% and 70%. The 35% royalty applies to sales in any territories. The 70% option applies to the territories of Andora, Austria, Belgium, Canada, France, Germany, Italy, Liechtenstein, Luxembourg, Monaco, San Marino, Switzerland, Spain, and the United Kingdom including Guernsey—Jersey and Isle-of-Man, the United States and the Vatican City.

If you have chosen 70%, then sales outside of the above territories will be paid at the 35% royalty rate.

If you select the 70% option, you should also note that the list price on Amazon must be at least 20% lower than any other publisher offering the digital or physical version of your book.

If you have an eBook that is mainly from Public Domain work, you can only expect to receive the 35% option.

Amazon does have a minimum and maximum price list. If you select the 35% option your book must be priced between a certain set amounts (the minimum price is higher if your book is greater than 3mb in size).

You need to consider what an appropriate price for a book is in your chosen category. This will have shown up in the research you did earlier before you commence writing your book.

If you price your book too low, then you may find it is not taken as a credible offering within the category, if you price your book too high you may find you simply are too expensive compared to your competitors.

Amazon allows you to update the pricing on your book at any time once it has been published, but bear in mind it can take up to 24 hours for a price change to become effective.

If you plan on selling your work on other platforms, make sure you have done your research very well so that you will know ahead of time the initial selling price for your book on various sites across the web.

Other publishing tips

The Kindle guidelines are easy to follow to ensure you have a good-quality book to publish there. Others, who have published on Kindle simply love it and I'm loving it too. The biggest selling point for any book is going to be quality content. If the book is good, it will likely sell, although you need to get the word out there to get your book noticed in the way of book promotion. Get engaged with the social media as a way of spreading words around about your book. Check on Google for book bloggers in your niche, join them and invite them to get your book at a discounted price and request them to write a review after reading the book.

Here are a few other tips you might want to consider when publishing.

Freelancers for formatting

Although formatting can be done yourself, it can be very frustrating as you try to make sure everything is exactly right if you are not good at this. Freelancers are affordable like fiverr.com, freelancers.com, upwork.com and many others which you can research on the internet. The freelancers will gladly do this for you and can convert it to any format you like at a cheap price also. You will need to research and scale down good freelancers. Be sure to request to see their past works, references, testimonials and you can also chat with them via Skype before selecting the appropriate freelancer based on your interview with them. This is necessary to ensure you hire a good freelancer.

You might even decide to stick with fiverr.com alone, as there are many good freelancers on fiverr.com if only you are willing to do an extensive research and take time to read the reviews of previous users of their services.

Right category

You get to select the category for your eBook when you publish onto the Kindle platform. Make sure that you select the right category so that your book can reach the target audience. Remember that this is imperative to get right, because it controls where they will place your book and where it ranks. You have to select the right niche to reach your target market, so choose them carefully. Select the categories you feel readers in your niche will search under. You will see a step by step guide at the end of this chapter to guide you in enrolling and choosing the right category for your book.

Design and Refine Your Cover

You should optimize your cover for the thumbnail size of the Kindle store. Kindle readers like to browse titles of new releases. They will see your title and cover right away. It will determine if they find it interesting enough to click and download a sample. If your cover only looks good close up, then consider editing it so that it looks good in thumbnail size to catch browsers attention. Also, remember that it needs to look good and be readable in greyscale. Hire a good freelancer to make your book cover for you.

Sample selection

With anything you write this is important, you have to "WOW" your target audience with the first few pages to arouse interest at wanting to read the rest of the book by making a purchase. With Kindle, readers can actually download the sample pages and if they read the first few pages and it does not grab their interest, they will delete them. They may read 20 or more samples and only buy one or two books. They have to be hooked by those few pages, so make sure your content is interesting to make them make a purchase. As a good rule of thumb, make sure you have them hooked within the first five pages or they probably will have no interest in your book.

Author profile

Be sure you complete your author profile. If you're not sure how to do this effectively, you can use Author Central - http://authorcentral.amazon.com/. Here you can upload a picture of you, add your biography, and view and edit your bibliography. It will even help you create a blog. A blog is a way to directly speak to all of the readers. It only takes a few minutes of your time and it will allow the reader to know more about you and you can begin a rapport with your readers.

Other Publishing Notes:

Print-on-demand books

You can create a book that is available both in digital and in physical formats if you use Create Space. You can do this from the same Amazon.com page. The Create Space program is a member of the Amazon group of companies. For your benefit, it has a full selection of tools and services that will help you self-publish and you can also contract the physical (paperback) books to Amazon at a cost. By using it you can make your book available for sale to the many customers on Amazon.com as well as make them available to other channels. What makes it so nice is that your books will always be in stock and available for your customers without any hassle from having to print and ship as Amazon does all this for you. This second book of mine will be both digital and paperback.

Amazon Associates Program

If you join this program, you can earn a 4% more on each sale you drive. This program allows you to create custom links to your books. It also allows you to create interactive widgets. These help to present your book in a more qualified light. Each time a customer clicks on one of those links and they purchase your book, then you get an additional 4% for every sale you make. You can promote your book via your blog and use the blog to invite your readers to enroll in Amazon associates program to enable them promote your work too.

Backups

You never know when disaster can strike. Your computer could get a virus or even get destroyed or stolen. Don't just rely on your trusty laptop or PC to save your material, make backups of everything you do. Make sure you have at least one hard copy and make at least two different digital copies and keep them in different places, such as "Google Drive, Dropbox and on a USB.
If you do this, you will still have your eBook and can recover quickly if something happens.

Specials (non-fiction in particular)

Somewhere in your book, give your readers a little reward. It might be your free report, or it may be a discount on another book or product you have to offer or simply requesting them to connect with you via your blog by subscribing to your newsletter to give the opportunity to always send them free stuff. Give them your email too where they can email you to ask questions and make other requests. It is a simple way to say "thank you" that will cause the reader to remember you. Also, consider linking from your eBook to a squeeze page (aka name capture page) where the reader needs to enter his or her email address to collect that reward. This way you can build your own email mailing list which you can use to let your readers know about your new books.

Call to Action

The goal is to attract more readers to your site. Every hit to your site increases your search engine optimization and helps you rise in the Google search result pages. It's best if you can put it near the end like maybe the next-to-the last page. Make sure your site has a great "About You" section where they can learn more about you or the business you are writing about. Always include a picture as it makes it more personal.

Promoting your eBook

You have gone through all the writing and editing process. You have formatted your eBook properly and have a dynamite cover that will attract the eyes of potential customers, and you have published it on Kindle. Now you just sit back and wait for your sales to go up, right? NO! It is up to you to promote your book as if you do nothing but expecting sales to roll in, you have made a mistake. You have to let the world know about your book in the way of advertising.

There are so many services that you can pay to help increase your eBook's visibility. If you think you have a book with "best seller" potential, it might be well worth it to pay someone else. For most beginning writers however, it will save you more if you promote the book yourself.

Here are a few that you should consider using:

Social Media

Social media marketing is especially effective for marketing books, because people naturally love to talk about books they enjoy, and there are plenty of different avenues available for promotion. There are many pages, different groups and fan pages on Facebook alone that allow promotion of your books as long as you follow their rules, and not only do they allow promotion, they often encourage it. Even if you can't find any Facebook fan pages devoted to your genre, you can create one, it is that simple! Creating and maintaining a fan page is quick and easy, and it can be used for more than just promoting your book. (You can also use it to promote affiliate products and other products that you sell.)

Sites like Facebook, Twitter, LinkedIn, etc are very popular sites. Posts made on these social media sites are seen by a lot of people. If you don't have at least a Facebook account for yourself, you need to create one. They are self-explanatory to set up, and only take a few minutes to get up and running. You want to set it up so everyone can be your friend and view your page.

Once you have created your page, post about your book regularly. Get the word out about where it's published and post a link where they can go to buy it. You can also give free copies out to encourage your readers to leave you a review which will ultimately assist you to get more sales. If the reviews are positive and convincing, this will act as inducer to potential buyers who will likely make a purchase. Once you have grown a strong presence on these sites, more and more people will be drawn to your site and your book.

The object with social media is to maximize exposure. Just telling people is not enough. You need to link it to everywhere they can find it.

Facebook

Facebook is perhaps the single most powerful social website not only for authors but for any type of business that you are in. You should have a fan page specifically created by you as an author. You may also want to have fan pages for your book or book series. To take advantage of other fan pages, search for groups and fan pages devoted to your niche or genre, especially those that focus on books. You will need to check their rules, and if they allow self-promotion, please do promote your book. If they do not allow self-promotion, you can contact the administrator of the page if there is a way to promote your book on their page as they may be opened to paid promotion, or they may even offer to promote your book for free, more especially if you give them free copy or you allow them to do a free giveaway on their page.

Twitter

Twitter is another great tool for authors if you use it properly. You can't just tweet your books over and over again and expect people to pay attention. Tweet about other interesting things to engage and attract fans. Tweeting about a simple recipe, motivational quotes, words of wisdom (from my own experience) seems to attract a lot of re-tweeting and followers, from there you can tweet about your book. I do this a lot and this has increased my exposure and followers on Twitter. The fans can become your book ambassadors, promoting the books for you and re-tweeting. If you become personal friends with some of your fans, all you have to do is post a tweet and ask them to "re-tweet" it for you, otherwise will simply re-tweet without you asking because of the relationship you have built with them or when they really like what you have tweeted about. Twitter will also send you emails of those that liked your tweets, re-tweet and new followers.

Pinterest

Pinterest is a growing social platform which mostly focuses on sharing images. You can create pin boards on which you pin various images. You can create lists of books in your genre and pin your own book to it. You can also ask other people to "re-pin" your book. If you re-pin some of their images, they will be more than willing to re-pin yours. In addition to making lists of books, you can also create pin boards that feature things people who might read your book would like. For example, if your book is about weight loss, you can have pin boards like:

- Yoga for fitness
- Best work-out wear
- Cool running shoes
- Low calorie diet
- Best workout DVDs and more

You could link to your book in the description of every pin board, getting you a lot more exposure than you would otherwise get. Remember to share you pins and boards on Facebook, Twitter and elsewhere in order to get maximum exposure. A great way to do this is to use this site www.ifttt.com (If This Then That) as what you do on one social platform can be replicated automatically on other platforms with the use of IFTTT.

GoodReads and LibraryThing

Goodreads.com and Librarything.com are two social networks that focuses specifically on books. The sites are great for book promotion. In addition to holding giveaways there, you can visit the various groups and participate. Just be sure to read the rules in each individual group to find out what their rules are regarding author participation. Since group are individually managed, each one has specific rules, make sure you learn about the rules and adapt to it.

YouTube

YouTube videos are simple to do. You don't have to hire a professional to do it. You can create a short video, usually only about three minutes, introducing yourself and your new book and post it on YouTube. Everything that makes it catchy to a reader will work to attract them to watch your video and learn more.

Get yourself out there - When people think real authors are accessible to them, they love it. You can advertise times and time, have virtual question and answer sessions about the book.

Google Plus

Google Plus is also a very good platform to interact with people to get them to know about your books. Make a circle of friends, colleagues, interact with them on a regular basis, get the word out about your book, it will amaze you that you will connect with so many people who are in your niche within a short period of time. Google Plus also combines many of the features of Facebook (personal profiles, business pages, group/communities) and also Twitter where as I said above you can add people to lists, "circles" and follow them. An additional feature with potential for authors is "hangouts" where you can do live video chats.

More important also is that data from Google Plus is being integrated into Google's search engine which means that your activity there could have an influence on the amount of traffic that is flowing to your site through search results.

Instagram

Instagram is another platform that authors or anyone can use to promote their works. If you are not yet on Instagram, you are missing out greatly. It is an image sharing site and if you take time to learn how to use it, you can build your followers up within a little time. Start by posting quality/educative images on a daily basis with the use of hashtags. If you do it well, you will get a great number of followers. I just started with this platform about a month ago and since I have been posting only interesting images with no strings attached, I have been able to get a good number of followers and have started chatting with them to know their interests and other stuff. If you are not there yet, head over now to sign up.

Reviews for your Book (Good Reviews)

Complimentary Copies

Google search and find bloggers who review books. Send them complimentary copies of your book and ask them to review it.

Review Copies

Giving away free copies of your book in exchange for review is a great idea, but make sure you tell people they are not required to leave a review, and that if they do, their review should be completely unbiased and honest. Do not ask for a five-star review but simply state that honest and unbiased reviews are appreciated. You can find people who want review copies at a variety of places such as Kboards.com, goodreads.com and Facebook.

Giveaways

In addition to giving copies to people specifically for review purposes, you can also do giveaways in order to get more people to read and possibly review your book.

Inside the Book

Do not forget a very simple way to get people to leave reviews for your book. At the end of your book, simply include a note asking people to leave a review if they like the book. Many authors do not think about doing this, however a simple reminder does not hurt.

Bloggers

There are many book bloggers on the internet, just search on google, give them copies in exchange for an honest review. I have listed some bloggers site at the end of this book.

Bad Reviews:

Paid Reviews

Do not risk it by paying for reviews for your book. Many people do this on sites such as fiverr.com or other similar sites. If Amazon ever finds out that you have paid someone to review your book, you could possibly lose your entire account. Paid reviews are the biggest no-no as far as reviews is concerned.

Good Reviews in Exchange for a Copy

While it is fine to give away copies of your book and ask people to please give you an honest review on Amazon, after they have read it, however, it is not okay to ask for or demand a five-star rating or positive reviews. Therefore, when giving away free copies, always state that you want an unbiased honest review of the book.

Exchanging Reviews with Authors

One popular method is for authors to give each other's books 5 star reviews in exchange for the other author doing the same in return. This is not a good practice. If Amazon discovers this happening, your reviews could be deleted and your account could be banned.

Careful with Purchased Services

When you are paying for editing or promoting, you want to make sure everything is clear and in writing. Sometimes deals sound so inexpensive, and end up costing you a fortune. If you can't determine what the final cost will be, don't use the service. Find someone you feel comfortable with and you can understand all the fine print.

You can also write another small eBook or report and offer it for free—Everyone likes to get free things. If you offer something free to either your subscribers or those who view your site, you will attract more traffic to your site. Many opt not to do this, because they think writing a report is just too difficult. It is really quite simple if you follow these simple steps:

1. Use a simple word processing program like MS Word.

2. Gather several articles you have written.

3. Select a few you feel go together and put them in an order that will make sense to the reader.

4. Make sure each concept flows with the next concept.

5. Find ways to connect them.

6. Have good sized margins of at least one inch on both the right and left. This will make it easier for people to read.

7. Make sure all the articles are in the same font. You want to use at least 11-12 point fonts because people of all ages need that to be able to read the book. Both Arial, Helvetica and Verdana have been found easier to read than Times New Roman.

8. You have created something simple and effective that you can give away in a few hours' time. It will attract people to you when they're looking for your topic and see that it's "FREE." Then, you can have the link on your site where they can buy your book. If you do a good report, this will be interested enough for readers to take a look at your book and if they like the way it looks, they will likely buy.

Once you have done all that, you have a product you can share with possible affiliate programs to help you promote your product in return for a commission, or for your promoting their product on your site. As long as the two are complimentary, it usually works well.

Tracking Your Kindle Sales

Knowing how much you sell on Amazon is probably very important to you, especially if it's your first book and you're all excited about it. There are several ways on Amazon to monitor your sales. If you have print books Amazon has ordered through you or if you have a Kindle Direct account, you can track in real time.

Direct Real Time

You can check your sales updates reports through both Kindle Direct Publishing and Amazon Advantage programs. All you have to do is log onto your account. You can check out your account as often as you want. Once a day is common, but you may want to check it once a week, a month or as you like.

Other publishers often only give you monthly statements and they send them about three weeks into the next month, so it takes a long time to actually see your results. With Amazon, you can even track print sales through many of their features. They always offer ways to estimate your sales.

Indirect Tracking

Indirectly, you can track your real-time sales in two ways. These are either by tracking the in-stock numbers or you can do it by tracking sales rank. You can find both of these on your Amazon book page. That is the page all of your potential customers can view. These numbers won't mirror your sales exactly, but they can give you a good idea of how well your sales are going.

Since Amazon has a very large number of books, they can't keep inventory of books that are slow sellers. If you have a self-published book, it probably falls into that category. Because of this, they will stock just enough as they anticipate your sales to be during that period of time. They base it on previous sales and only reorder when the inventory is low.

They do, however, entice people who browse to buy the book with statements like, "Order soon, only 2 left in stock." This helps you in tracking. You can check to see if the inventory is changing at all.

You can use the in-stock numbers to let you know how many they have in stock. It will say something like "10 New in stock now" when they order new books from the distributor. There are a few disadvantages to using the in-stock statistical method.

For instance, they will only list the number left in stock when that number is low. If you don't know how many they ordered in the first place, you cannot figure out how many books they have sold. Also, you can only use the "in stock" number if you have a printed book. If your book is an eBook, you can't track this way at all. If you use the Amazon Best Sellers Rank, you can also indirectly track sales. You just have to scroll down until you find your book. There will be a separate page for paperback, hardcover, and Kindle. Find the Product Details section. Go to the end of it, and you can see what your sales rank is for your book.

You should know that this is not based on just sales of your book. It also takes into account sales of all books that are in that category. If you see 1,000, that's awesome, but a ranking of 100,000 might not be the best, you need to do more in form of advert to ensure you have a good ranking.

If other books in your category are selling quickly and yours are not, your number goes up instead of down, that is not what you want. Your rank goes up when you have more sales relative to the category than other books and the ranking is done on an hourly basis. You should also set up an Author Central account, which is simple to do and it will let you see sales information that no one else can see.

Another way is by the Nielsen Book Scan. You can find this in the Amazon Author Central tools which give you data for sales of printed books for a period of 4 – 8 weeks.

The Book Scan report enables authors to learn about their sales close to the time they occur. It is a useful tracking tool if the company that produced your book does not post sales for a month or two. Both Kindle Direct Publishing and Amazon Advantage programs continuously update sales reports, which you can easily access by logging into your account. You can log into your Kindle account at least once a every week when you have an ad running or a new guest blog post that mentions your books.

Other promotion company report contents monthly and run about three months into the next month before you see last month's reports. This causes you not to see your reports for sometimes two months. This makes it difficult at best to track. You can, however, indirectly track print sales through several Amazon features, which offer ways to estimate recent sales. Author Central also provides graphs of your Amazon Best Sellers Rank history for the past four or eight weeks. The separate graphs for each format of your book offer a visual way to compare print and e-book performance.

Information and Promotional Purposes

I have discussed how important the entire process is from beginning to end, everything has to be given your very best work and care. I can't stress enough, however, that creating the perfect book means nothing if you don't take an active part in promoting your book. There are various types of promotion listed in this book, and you should definitely begin to explore each and find out more ways to get your book out there.

Try a few different methods at the same time and alternate them frequently. Soon, you will find the one, or group of ones that will work for you. Remember to get yourself out there. Do guest blog posting, google hangouts and much more. You can often find affiliates who will have you interview them about the eBook and then they will offer to interview you about your book and future plans. Blog posting, webinars, or even mentions of friends public sites can do you the world of good. Then if you add a paid advertisement to the mix, tracking sales results is an excellent way to learn which methods work best.

Viewing your Promotion Results

At a time when you are not doing any promotion, follow your sales figures to establish a baseline. The sales during this period can probably be attributed to word of mouth and search engine hits rather than your intentional efforts.

Be especially watchful in tracking your sales when you are paying for an ad or other type of promotion. A potential customer may not stop what he/she is doing to order a book but will wait until a convenient time to do so. Follow the sales of all of your book's formats. You may have linked to the Kindle version, but a reader may prefer a print copy.

You may often find an increase in your sales if you have a guest blog. They often come through self-run ads. You can Google your title to see if your book is mentioned. If you don't see something, then do it again. Look at all the search results and see if you can even find a mention of your book. If you can't find anything much or nothing at all, this means you need to buck up. I'm talking from experience here as I have not been doing much and hence did not really see any results. But once I incorporate what I'm teaching you here, I began to have friends, engage them with what I do, and the result is encouraging now and I'm sure I will get there soon if I cannot this way. Sometimes you may see where someone has asked a question on a blog or twitter remark, if you have, take the time to respond and even thank them as a way of appreciating them, as it works.

Plan Future Promotions

Now that you know all about your promotion efforts and how they have led to sales, you are ready to do more. You can plan better now how to spend the balance of your money and your important time you can plan how best to spend your time and money promoting your book. Guest blogging, hangouts or even webinars will not always generate great sales for your books, but they do allow you to put the titles of your books into visitors' minds, take little effort, and cost nothing. In other words, you may not have gained much by doing it, but you did not lose anything either and you will have gained a handful of friends that can later translate into buyers.

When it comes to an ad that is paid that is a different story. If you don't see an upward flow in sales, you may think twice before continuing or repeating the advertisement.

Keep track of your sales over time. Look at your sales closely to see if they peak in certain months. If they do, then you will want to remember those months in which they peak, concentrate your promotion to hit buyers at or just before the peak.

Amazon Contract Services

Amazon doesn't just sign you up and forget about you. They have given you the tools you need to help you publish your new eBooks. They offer you the use of their tools to help you get your eBook published. With the continued rise of all the many social networking sites, it opens up the world to have the opportunity to view your eBook. You also receive KPD Newsletters every month, where you will read about the success story of other authors, what you can do to make your book better and more.

There will never be such a type of available/free or minimal cost advertising for which you can promote. If you have a problem with anything in the book publishing process, Amazon KDP has help sheets to help you. They also have good customer care service, so simply contact them and explain what problems you have had and they will help you to correct them. Amazon is ever ready 24 – 7 to help and sort you out, it is really a great platform to use for your digital and paperback books. Once you join the platform, you will always receive monthly newsletters of what is happening in the Kindle world, advise from other authors, what you can do to have more readers for your book and many other useful suggestions.

I have said earlier that you can have your royalty via electronic fund transfer or check, however, I just received an email and thank heavens, this book has not been published as the rules have now changed. Royalty henceforth will only be paid via electronic funds transfer, while issuing of checks is now restricted.

Good luck with your writing.

I have set down below step by step guide on how to enroll your book on the Kindle platform.

Here's how to publish your book on Amazon Kindle's bookstore.

Step 1: Sign In

Go to:

https://kdp.amazon.com

This is Amazon's Kindle self-publishing platform. If you are new, you will need to register and login to the site as indicated above.

Step 2: Click Add New Title

Once you are in your KDP account, click "Add New Title" to begin the process of adding your new Kindle book.

Introducing KDP Select

Introducing KDP Select - a new option to make money and promote your book. When you r
90 days, it will be part of the Kindle Owners' Lending Library for the same period and you wi
readers borrow your books from the library. You will also be able to promote your book as fr
Learn more

Step 3: KDP Select

Do you want to enroll in KDP select? KDP select allows you to share in library
revenues when

people borrow your book, as well as to offer your book for free on the Kindle
store for 5 days. In

order to enroll in KDP select, you will need to offer your book only on the
Amazon Kindle and no other digital platform.

Introducing KDP Select

Introducing KDP Select - a new option to make money and promote your book. When you make your book exclusive to Kindle for at least 90 days, it will be part of the Kindle Owners' Lending Library for the same period and you will earn your share of a monthly fund when readers borrow your books from the library. You will also be able to promote your book as free for up to 5 days during these 90 days. Learn more

☐ **Enroll this book in KDP Select**

By checking the box, you are enrolling in KDP Select. Books enrolled in KDP Select must not be available in digital format on any other platform during their enrollment. See the KDP Select Terms and Conditions for more details.

Step 4: Book Title

Here, you will enter the title of your book. There are a few things you should be thinking about when you choose a title:

The title should be catchy and if someone hears the name, it should immediately get stuck in their head.

The title should suggest a benefit as this will help people know what will get from reading your book.

It should be unique; this means you should avoid using a generic title that others have used so many times.

It should catch attention, and if potential buyers are looking at your book in the Kindle store, the title should draw their attention and arouse their curiosity.

1. Enter Your Book Details

Book name:

Freelance Writing Guide|

Please enter the exact title only. Books submitted with extra words in this field will not be published. (Why?)

Step 5: Enter Your Description

Your description is the best chance to sell your book and make someone interested at reading your content. The headline should catch attention and the cover should help in building a vibe and brand as people ultimately decides whether or not they want to buy your book after reading the description. Therefore, the description should focus on the reader and explain how your book can change their lives or benefit them in some way. This should highlight the juiciest aspects of your book. To get a good description, write it before hand, read it out loud and listen carefully to how it sounds to you and if it sounds well, I'm sure your target audience will find it attractive too.

☐ This book is part of a series (What's this?)

Series title: Volume:

Edition number (optional): (What's this?)

2

Description: (What's this?)

Learn how to earn an income writing for yourself or for other people. Step by step illustrated guide.

3899 characters left

Step 6: Publisher Details

Here, you will have to enter details about the publisher. Most of this information is optional, but it does help lend sense of credibility to your book. Note that to publish on Kindle store, you do not need an ISBN number.

Book contributors: (What's this?)

[Add contributors]

Language: (What's this?)
English ▾

Publication date (optional):
05/17/2012

Publisher (optional): (What's this?)
Penguin Books

ISBN (optional): (What's this?)
863232489465451

Step 7: Publishing Rights

You have to verify with Amazon that you have the rights to publish the book you want to publish

2. Verify Your Publishing Rights

Publishing rights status: (What's this?)

○ This is a public domain work.

○ This is not a public domain work and I hold the necessary publishing rights.

Step 8: Categories and Keywords

Click "Add Categories" to add categories. Enter your keywords in the keywords section.

Your categories and your keywords are some of the most important aspects of getting found.

Customers will browse books by categories as well as search for books using keywords.

If you don't know which categories or keywords you should use, look into what some of your competitors are using. You can't go wrong doing what your top 5 competitors are doing in terms of categories and keywords.

3. Target Your Book to Customers

Categories (What's this?)

[Add categories]

Search keywords (up to 7, optional): (What's this?)

> Writing, freelancing|

5 keywords left

This is what the category selection screen looks like:

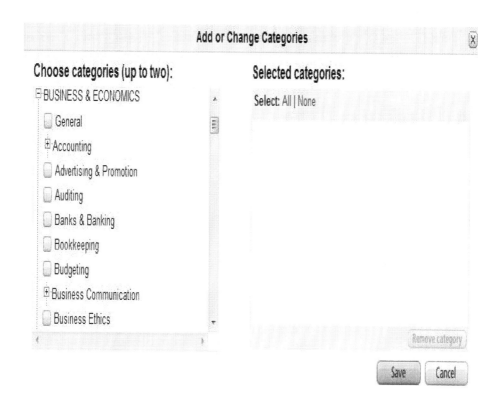

Step 9: Upload Your Book

You need to check whether or not you want to enable Digital Rights Management (DRM) to help protect your book from being shared and/or pirated.

Then upload your book's contents by clicking "Browse for Book" then "Upload Book."

5. Upload Your Book File

Select a digital rights management (DRM) option: (What's this?)

○ Enable digital rights management

○ Do not enable digital rights management

Book content file:

[   ]   Browse for book...

> Learn KDP content guidelines   Upload book
> Help with formatting

Once Amazon receives your book, you will see the converting screen as shown below.

 Converting book file to Kindle format...

This may take a few moments. If you have completed all required fields above, click "Save and Continue" to move forward while conversion continues.

Click "Save and Continue" to continue with the book creation process.

Step 10: Publishing Territories

If you only hold the rights to the book in certain territories, you will have to restrict the sales to just those territories, however, most publishers leave this option on "Worldwide rights".

7. Verify Your Publishing Territories

Select the territories for which you hold rights: (What's this?)

⦿ Worldwide rights - all territories

◯ Individual territories - select territories

Select: All | None

United States

United Kingdom

Guernsey

Isle Of Man

Jersey

Canada

Step 11: Royalty Options

Choose which royalty option you want to use to promote your book as Amazon has two different

royalty plans that you can choose from. If you are selling or setting your price between $2.99 to $9.99, the 70% option is probably your best choice. However, if you are selling for $0.99 then the 35% option is your only choice.

8. Choose Your Royalty

Please select a royalty option for your book. (What's this?)

○ 35% Royalty

◉ 70% Royalty

Step 12: Set Your Prices

Set the prices for your book in various different markets. When you are setting your prices, try to

take a look at what your competitors are charging in those markets before you make your decision.

It is not unusual for a book that sells for $2.99 USD to sell for £2.99 GBP, even though the

pound is worth $1.58 dollars, this is just how the market works. In other words, don't just convert your US dollar prices into pounds or euros, instead, research each market before crafting your prices.

	List Price	Royalty Rate	Delivery Costs	Estimated Royalty
Amazon.com	$ 2.99 USD Must be between $2.99 and $9.99	35% 70%	n/a $0.06	$1.05 $2.05
Amazon.co.uk	☐ Set UK price automatically based on US price £ 1.99 GBP Must be between £1.49 and £7.81	70%	£0.04	£1.36
Amazon.de	☐ Set DE price automatically based on US price € 2.99 EUR Must be between €2.60 and €9.70	70%	€0.05	€2.06
Amazon.fr	☐ Set FR price automatically based on US price € 2.99 EUR Must be between €2.60 and €9.70	70%	€0.05	€2.06

Step 13: Should you allow lending?

If you want to use this option so that people should be able to "lend" your book to their friends, or colleagues then you will have to enroll in KDP lending library. This will enable the readers to give the book to someone else for 14 days and Amazon will automatically deactivate the book after the two weeks has passed. Some authors believe this helps to increase their brand and exposure, while others believe it decreases potential revenue, the ball is in your court to decide whether you want to do this or not.

9. Kindle Book Lending

☑ Allow lending for this book (Details)

Step 14: Save and Publish

Once you have entered all the details for your book and selected all your publishing options, just click "Save and Publish" to finalize your submission!

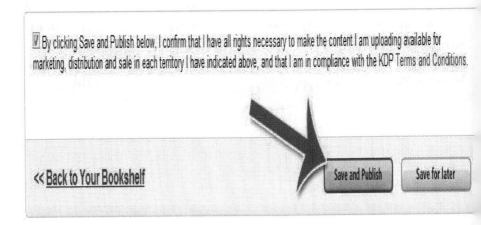

By clicking Save and Publish below, I confirm that I have all rights necessary to make the content I am uploading available for marketing, distribution and sale in each territory I have indicated above, and that I am in compliance with the KDP Terms and Conditions.

<< Back to Your Bookshelf   Save and Publish   Save for later

Approval will take some time as your book will be reviewed by Amazon to ensure it is your handwork. If you write the book yourself, you will almost get approved quick as Amazon's only primary reason for disapproving book has to do with copyright issues.

FINAL WORD

My final word will be that once you finish this book, put into pen and paper your action plans daily, weekly, quarterly and yearly. If you simply read this book and put it down without taking any actions, nothing will change. If, however, you are serious even before you finish this book, I expect you to have a pen/paper with which you will jot down the lessons/ideas you have gained so that you will be able to have an itemized list of what you plan to do, and how you will achieve it.

With all said and done, make sure you register for Amazon's various webinars so that you can learn how to be successful in any of its program you choose. From time to time also, make sure you watch the videos on Amazon's site, read all about the information that will enable you to become successful in any of the various ways in which you can make money from Amazon.

Finally, once you register with Amazon, the online giant retailer never leaves you alone as you will always receive updates from them on how to take your business to the next level.

You can connect with me via my blog (http://www.thesources.co.uk) or email me estherb@live.co.uk for any help or assistance, I'm always available.

If you enjoyed this book, please do not forget to leave me a review, thank you.

To your success.

Esther

ABOUT THE AUTHOR

I am Esther B. Odejimi, a graduate of the University of Greenwich and relocated from Nigeria to the United Kingdom in 2007. I have always wanted to work for myself, which was one of the main reasons why I migrated to the United Kingdom. Through research on the Internet, I stumbled upon several ways an individual can work from home as an alternative to 9 – 5 day job, which I never liked anyway. I tried most of the systems that I came across, but failed miserably and lost countless amounts of money - until I came across Amazon and eBay as a potential way a person can earn money from the two sites working from home by selling.

I got started with Amazon first and registered to become a seller. My first sales came from the books that I had earlier purchased from the site that I didn't need any longer and resold them. I was shocked to see that I sold all of the books within a short period of time. I continued to source for books to sell, since these were the only items I knew how to sell until I researched additional ways on how to become a big seller on Amazon; this allowed me to add other categories by buying other items aside from books.

As sales continued to increase across the Amazon marketplace, profits began to take a dive since the competition was very fierce. I began deep research again on how to overcome the competition and I found a coach/mentor that really understood how to keep the competitors at bay and sell with peace on Amazon. This is when I found out about Product Label Rights (PLR) of physical products. At the time of writing this book, I have entered into the private label. Now that I have my own products, it is easy for me to decide the price I want to sell my items with no stiff competition from other sellers. I have also enrolled into Amazon Associates program (affiliate marketing) and selling digital products via reputable platforms like Fiverr, JV Zoo and just about adding Teachable and Clickbank to the list.

As soon as I began to succeed in selling again, I ventured into writing books and selling them through the Kindle Publishing Program - this is my second book which will be in both Kindle format and paperback. There is a lot of money to be made from writing books if only you know what to write about (this boils down to research of what book people are ready to read and buy). You are not reinventing any wheel, you just learn what others are doing and look for ways to make it better. Even if you don't know how to write a book, you can still become an author as there are so many ways in which you can hire freelancers who could ghostwrite for you. It is easy for me to write my book as I can type very fast (I used to be a Secretary in my early years). All I need to do is to write up how I want the book to be in terms of headings and chapters, the rest is history as I type while at the same time thinking the processes through. I'm already working on a third book which will be out soon.

Finally, I'm married and live happily with my family. I'm a firm believer in God as I believe He created me in His own image and after His likeness to fulfill His purpose on earth. Without Him, I'm incomplete and continually give Him all the glory for what I have been able to do and achieve so far.

Suggested Amazon Resource Tools for Sellers

FBA Revenue Calculator
https://sellercentral.amazon.co.uk/hz/fba/profitabilitycalculator/index?lang=en_GB

Merchant Words
https://www.merchantwords.com

AMZ Tracker
https://www.amztracker.com/

Google Trends
https://www.google.com/trends/

Google Keyword Tool
https://adwords.google.com/KeywordPlanner

CamelCamelCamel
http://uk.camelcamelcamel.com/

Simple Keyword Inspector
http://www.keywordinspector.com/.

AMZ Shark
https://amzshark.com/

Junglescout
http://www.junglescout.com/

Wholesalers/Suppliers

Alibaba
http://www.alibaba.com/

Aliexpress
http://www.aliexpress.com/

Wholesale Alibaba
http://wholesaler.alibaba.com/

Global sources
http://www.globalsources.com/

ECVV
http://www.ecvv.com/

DH Gate
http://www.dhgate.com/

Light in the box
http://www.lightinthebox.com/

Made in China
http://www.madeinchina.com/

Book Bloggers

Book Blogging
http://bookblogging.net

Candaces book blog
http://www.candacesbookblog.com/

Katie's Book Blog
http://katiesbookblog.com/

The Book Bloggers List
http://bookbloggerlist.com/

The Indie Review
http://www.theindieview.com/

Printed in Great Britain
by Amazon